THE LAY CONTEMPLATIVE

■ TESTIMONIES

■ PERSPECTIVES

■ RESOURCES

Edited by **VIRGINIA MANSS**

and **MARY FROHL**

Forewor

ST. ANTHONY MESSENGER PRESS

Cincinnati, Ohio

Scripture citations are taken from the *New Revised Standard Version of the Bible*, copyright ©1989, by the Division of Christian Education of the National Council of the Churches of Christ in the USA. Used with permission. All rights reserved.

The excerpt from *The Essential Rumi*, translated by Coleman Barks, copyright ©1995, is reprinted by permission of Threshold Books.

The excerpt from *Lame Deer: Seeker of Visions* by John Fire Lame Deer and Richard Erodes, copyright ©1972 by John Fire Lame Deer and Richard Erodes, is reprinted with the permission of Pocket Books, a division of Simon & Schuster, Inc.

Excerpts from *Quaker Spirituality: Selected Writings*, edited and introduced by Douglas V. Steere, copyright ©1984 by Douglas V. Steere, and *Vatican II: Assessment and Perspectives* (Vol. I) edited by Rene Latourelle, copyright ©1988 by Rene Latourelle, are reprinted with the permission of Paulist Press.

Excerpts from *Voluntary Simplicity* by Duane Elgin, copyright ©1993, are used by permission of Wm. Morrow & Co., Inc.

The excerpt from *Plain and Simple* by Sue Bender, copyright ©1989, is used by permission of HarperCollins Publishers.

The excerpt from *Maenads, Martyrs, Matrons, Monastics: A Sourcebook on Women's Religions in the Greco-Roman World*, ed. Ross S. Kraemer, copyright ©1988, is used by permission of the author.

The excerpt from *The Selected Poetry of Rainer Maria Rilke*, ed. and trans. Stephen Mitchell, copyright ©1982 by Stephen Mitchell, is reprinted by permission of Random House, Inc.

Cover and book design by Constance Wolfer

ISBN 0-86716-370-4

Copyright ©2000, The Association of Contemplative Sisters
All rights reserved.

Published by St. Anthony Messenger Press

Printed in the U.S.A.

Contents

Foreword

by Tilden Edwards, Shalem Institute

In 1973 I found myself searching for help with my spiritual life. Very few of the resources I discovered then really fit the particular calling that I was sensing inside me. That calling is what this book names as contemplation in the ordinary world. The resources available for this calling at that time were largely monastic. Even in the monastic communities I visited, though, I often sensed the beginnings of an enlarged appreciation of contemplative living in the non-monastic world. Since that time, some of the monks in these communities have been leaders in fostering new versions of contemplative practice for people living ordinary lives in the world.

If I were beginning to look for resources for contemplative living in the world today, I would find a lot more available to me. Unfortunately, it is still difficult to discover these resources and to know exactly how they might be relevant to my situation. One of the great contributions of this book is the way it brings together for the first time a practical description of a great many of these resources, based on firsthand visits by the authors. For lay people searching for assistance in deepening and supporting their contemplative calling, these carefully described resources can be an invaluable resource.

And there are many such lay people around today! The marks of the contemplative call, I believe, include such things as a sense of divine immediacy, a call to live out of that immediacy and a sense of all things and events as transparencies for divine presence. Particular practices such as silence and solitude are meant to help us appreciate that presence through all interior and exterior phenomena. This graced appreciation is a hidden wellspring that helps cleanse the moment of the fears and grasping that obscure the divine presence. Then God's Spirit can more easily flow through us with its bouyant love and wisdom.

Such qualities of presence are desperately needed in our time. Some people are gifted and called to cultivate these qualities in great depth, leading them to greater communion with God and with all that is of God in the world. I think everyone, though, is called at least to an occasional encounter with these qualities and their fruits. They belong to the very nature of our souls and reveal the deepest ground of our unity. As someone once said, a contemplative isn't a special kind of person, everyone is a special kind of contemplative. In this sense, as the Preface points out, we are all lay people, part of the *laos*, the people of God, before we're distinguished by particular callings. Some people, though, do find a special contemplative orientation at the core of their daily lives. The resources in this book can be of value to both "full" and "partial" contemplatives.

Lay contemplatives in the world often live and work among people who do not share their sense of contemplative orientation. Without an ordered community to affirm what is important to them, those with the calling to be contemplatives in the world can feel hidden and lonely. Such people often crave the company of others who are oriented as they are. I have seen people come to programs at the Shalem Institute who feel such an enormous relief to be able to speak freely about their interior lives and yearnings without worrying that they may be seen as crazy or alien.

Besides the helpful descriptions of specific contemplative resource centers, the other special contribution of this book is the way it gives many mature lay people a chance to talk about their concrete experience of living contemplatively oriented lives in the world. Some of these offerings provide deep insight into the nature and formation of a contemplative orientation in today's world. These contributions can be of great value to those many people who seek not only contemplative company, but further opportunities for support in responding to the ever-evolving call to drop deeper into the undefinable subtlety of the living Presence.

Lay contemplatives are hidden leaven throughout the worlds of family, work, community, church, friendships, the arts and social action. Their influence as witnesses and transparencies for the larger Presence is a vital avenue of grace in the world. They deserve every kind of encouragement and support possible. This book is a great contribution to the recognition, affirmation and resourcing of this motley band of precious people. Through them thousands of others become aware of that hidden contemplative streak that belongs to our inmost being.

Preface

by Mary Frohlich and Virginia Manss

In our times more and more people, from all circumstances of life, are finding themselves drawn to the serious pursuit of contemplation. A number of recent books have offered personal stories and models for these contemplatives "outside the boundaries." This book aims to go a step further, providing within a single volume a variety of resources that will assist the Christian layperson in deepening a contemplative vocation. Despite their diversity, these resources converge upon a single vision: support for the flourishing of the seeds of the contemplative charism that have not landed in the soil of cloistered gardens, but rather are seeking to put down roots near the busy highways of secular life.

The idea for the book emerged in the course of a five-year research project by the Association of Contemplative Sisters (ACS) on the "Formation of Christian Lay Contemplatives." The project began in 1992 when ACS, an association of contemplative women from all walks of life, formed a Task Force. The group applied to the Lilly Endowment and received a small grant to support a survey of the ACS membership on this topic (see Appendix B). Later, another small grant made it possible to collate and distribute the results. Subsequent to that, a larger Lilly grant was awarded to support the preparation of this book.

■ TERMINOLOGICAL CONTROVERSIES

From the beginning of this research project, it has been evident that each word in our ad hoc title could be problematic and controversial. *Formation, lay, contemplative* and even *Christian*—each term carries the freight of history in a way that often makes it ambiguous or, for some hearers, even negative. It seems as if entering upon an exploration of lay contemplation involves crossing some of the major minefields in contemporary ecclesial life. For example, reference to interest in "contemplatives" often seems to arouse anxieties that someone, or someone's spirituality, is going to be unjustly denigrated by not being included in this category. The addition of the word *lay* does not help. Some express confusion about what this combination might refer to, while others are concerned that it reinforces distinctions that they would rather see minimized. Because of the importance of this issue for our project, a brief reflection on the meaning of laity is provided here in the preface; Mary Frohlich's essay, "A Roman Catholic Theology of Lay Contemplation"(page 45), includes a more in-depth discussion.

Such terminological concerns are not trivial; they have significant basis both in the contemplative experience itself and in contemporary theology. No matter what position one takes on some of these issues, it is likely to be disturbing to some readers. We—the editors and others who have worked on the project—are aware that our own horizons are limited, and that neither individually nor collectively can we claim to speak for others. Nevertheless, we have tried—and we encourage others to try—to keep the focus where it belongs, on helping to shape an intellectual, spiritual and practical world within which many varieties of Christian contemplatives can flourish. In that bigger picture the selection and contextualization of terminology is significant, but not the central concern. ˙

■ WHO ARE THE 'LAITY' ADDRESSED BY THIS BOOK?

Among Roman Catholics, the most common way of using the term *layperson* is to refer to someone who is neither ordained nor a member of a canonical religious community. Recent research, however, critiques that usage and asserts that both biblically and theologically, it is more accurate to derive the term *laity* from the Greek *laos tou theou*, "people of God." In this view all the baptized are *laos*; it is a positive term for the fundamental Christian state of life, rather than a negative term for those without certain specified ministries or charisms. It is probably for this reason that the term has played a much smaller role in Protestant self-understanding, since one of the founding concerns of Protestantism was to downplay life-style differences between ministers and other Christians.

Within Christian reflection, then, the term *lay* can carry two different connotations. First, it can refer to the basic condition of all the baptized "people of God." Second, it can refer to the distinct condition of those who are not clergy or religious. There is tension between these meanings—and, not surprisingly, there is also ongoing theological and ecclesiastical controversy over these definitions and their implications. In this book we try to let the dual meaning of *lay* be a richness, rather than simply a confusion. Insofar as "lay contemplative" refers to any baptized person who is drawn to contemplation and seeks to live it within the reality of everyday life "in the world," the resources in this book can be of assistance to a wide range of such persons—including clergy and religious. On the other hand, the particular focus of attention is on those who enter upon a contemplative vocation without the benefit of the practical support and identity that religious community and/or priestly ordination are designed to supply. Our use of the term "lay contemplative" embraces both connotations.

In light of this, perhaps something needs to be said about the fact that many of the resources presented here have deep roots in the experience of religious communities. It is often said these days that lay spirituality should not be derived from models proper to religious life. True enough—but we must be careful not to interpret that too dualistically, as if Christian lay life and Christian religious life had nothing to do with one another. In fact, the roots of the vast majority of religious communities are in "lay contemplation"—a profound, charismatic experience of the Spirit that moved a group of lay women or men to drastically reorder their lives around the imperative of union with God. One implication of this is that some of today's lay contemplatives may eventually be led to become founders and foundresses of new forms of religious life. Another implication, however, is that all the laity have an equal claim as rightful heirs to the hard-earned wisdom of all Christian contemplatives, whatever their state of life.

For example: While most laity cannot immerse themselves for months or years at a time in a monastic life-style (and many would not even want to), a great many find briefer immersions, or the adaptation of selected monastic practices, very compatible with their "secular" contemplative way. It is true, of course, that new practices, not developed primarily within the framework of religious life, need to be discovered and encouraged; but to arbitrarily cut out of consideration the heritage of contemplative practice within religious communities would not be a service to the nurturance of contemporary lay contemplatives.

■ THE CONTENTS OF THE BOOK

The original inspiration for the book was awareness of an urgent need to help lay contemplatives find ways to receive preparation and nurturance in living that vocation. Members of the Association of Contemplative Sisters were sensitive to this need, since many have themselves endured great loneliness and uncertainty in responding to the calling that lies so deep and yet has so often been unsupported by external structures. Much of the energy of our original research went into what is now Part Three of the book: reports on centers for lay contemplative formation. More background on this section is contained in its own introduction.

As the task force reflected on the project, we realized that a real guidebook would need to include other sections as well. The first to be added was Part Two, which consists of several essays providing a variety of theological, philosophical and practical guidelines for growing as a lay contemplative.

Mary Frohlich's first piece, "A Roman Catholic Theology of Lay Contemplation," reflects on contemporary theological insights into theological anthropology, ecclesiology and Christology that have implications for the spirituality of lay contemplatives. Stephen K. Hatch's "The Formation of the Everyday Contemplative" reviews basic contemplative practices. Frohlich's second essay, "Lonely Valleys and Strange Islands: Contemplative Conversations With the 'Other,'" offers suggestions for how to come to terms with the often confusing array of spiritualities that await the contemplative seeker in today's world. Finally, Wendy M. Wright has provided some practical and theological guidelines for discernment.

Part One, "The Lay Contemplative Experience," came last but in some ways is the key to the whole book. As we reviewed the materials we were collecting, we realized that the real-life experience of lay contemplatives was the missing piece. We asked a number of people to write short reflections, encouraging them to focus on one or two vignettes that can give a flavor of this way of life. The six pieces that are offered here are powerful testimonies to the authenticity of this vocation, as well as to its many faces.

In soliciting the essays for Parts One and Two, we made an attempt to include authors from a variety of backgrounds and life-styles. Of the authors for Part Two, Stephen Hatch and Wendy Wright are both married and are raising children, while Mary Frohlich recently joined a religious community. Wright and Frohlich are Roman Catholic; Hatch has an eclectic religious identity that is centered in Quakerism and Buddhism. From Part One, Jonas, the Dundens and Denham are married, while Scott, Damiano and Durback are single. Among these, all are Roman Catholic except Damiano, who is Quaker.

Despite the fact that we made some efforts to include perspectives other than that of our own Roman Catholic communion, the book is by no means representative of the full range of Christian life. Most of the authors—and, indeed, most of the formation sites that were studied—are Roman Catholic. To some degree this reflects the fact that the language and practices of contemplation have a longer public history in that tradition. As well, the historical roots of the sponsoring organization, the Association of Contemplative Sisters, are Roman Catholic. ACS is now ecumenical, yet a high percentage of the membership still consists of women of Roman Catholic heritage. Finally, the focus may simply be a function of our own limited horizons. We encourage future researchers to press further in the search for diverse expressions of contemplative life.

■ CONCLUSION

Our inclusive understanding of laity (as well as of contemplation) means that any spiritual seeker may find support for his or her contemplative development in the resources and guidelines presented here. At the same time, one of the goals of the book is to define and foster the vocation of a less inclusive group, namely, those who experience a call to give contemplation a defining priority in their lives while living an "ordinary," secular Christian life. How large is that group? It is difficult to say. Our experience of being among lay contemplatives is that most are much more passionately concerned with opening up boundaries than with closing them down. Lay contemplatives are open to all fellow-travelers, and they do not place limits on where or among whom they will find them. The primary focus, therefore, should not be on inclusion and exclusion—"You are/are not a lay contemplative"—but on affirming, celebrating and understanding a vocation that some are struggling painfully to live, often with remarkably little support. In that spirit, we dedicate this book to everyone out there on the path, valiantly pursuing the contemplative way against all odds.

The Lay Contemplative Movement

by Mary Frohlich

Recently I participated in a retreat that was advertised as "Contemplative Intensive." The regime of the retreat included fifteen 25-minute periods of contemplative prayer each day, in addition to Mass and two work periods. We knew nothing about the identities of our fellow retreatants until the last day, when we all introduced ourselves and shared something of our contemplative experience. Of the forty people present that day, two were religious priests and ten or so were women religious. The remainder included parents, grandparents, carpenters, teachers, social workers, business people, secretaries, financial consultants—women and men of all ages and races, of widely varied ethnic and religious heritage.

As each person spoke, the most striking testimonies came from those who least reflected common stereotypes of contemplatives. A father of two young daughters spoke of how brushing his daughters' hair each morning had become a continuation of his preceding period of contemplative prayer. Another father talked about how remaining centered and clear-headed while dealing with three teenagers was his most significant contemplative practice. A retired secretary described the struggle she had gone through on the first day of the retreat as she tried to pray as she thought she ought to, and how a whole new simplicity of prayer had bloomed when she finally let go of expectations. A tall, elegant woman of about forty asked for prayers because, on the day the retreat began, she had resigned from her professional position and made a commitment to follow the contemplative path, wherever it might lead her.

These vignettes offer a glimpse of the burgeoning reality of lay contemplation. These people's lives are, in most respects, ordinary:

They raise families, do housework, earn a living, struggle with relational and career problems. At the same time, they have identified within themselves an urgency toward being contemplative. The specific discipline that this demands of each one varies; what is clear, however, is that each one feels deeply called and deeply committed.

The lay contemplative movement occurring today is in no way in opposition to the traditional, religious life expression of contemplative life. In fact, most lay contemplatives look to these communities for a significant portion of their support and companionship on the contemplative journey. Nevertheless, it is noteworthy that, as the new millennium dawns, many of the canonically established contemplative communities seem to be struggling to maintain both their numbers and their sense of fresh energy. In many cases, at least among women's communities, many of their "new" vocations are actually midlife transfers from other religious congregations. It is now quite rare for a young person to enter one of these communities and stay for more than four or five years.

Meanwhile, the lay contemplative movement is full of energy, creativity and new life. It is also often full of confusion, uncertainty and a bit of wildness—characteristics of youth. It remains to be seen what will come of all this. Even though some local monasteries have already been forced to close and others will certainly follow, there is little likelihood that deep-rooted traditions such as those of the Carmelites, Trappists and Poor Clares will die out. These traditions will continue to be rich sources of nurturance for seekers on the contemplative way. In the new millennium, however, we are also seeing the seedpods broken open and the gift of the contemplative vocation scattered abroad to bear fruit by every highway and byway.

■ WHAT IS 'OLD' ABOUT LAY CONTEMPLATION?

While some may assume that lay contemplation is a radically new phenomenon with practically no precedents in the past, the truth is considerably more nuanced. There is indeed something new about this movement, but, looking backward over the many generations of the Christian contemplative quest, we discover that, more fundamentally, it is the fruition of an impulse that has been present from the beginning of the Christian movement. Two movements in particular seem relevant to our own concerns.

In Christian history two of the most generative periods for the development of contemplative life—namely, the desert movements of the third to fifth centuries and the eremitical movements of the eleventh to thirteenth centuries—have been eras in which grassroots Christians took the lead. Each of these began as lay movements and, even as they evolved into more institutionalized forms of religious life, continued to inspire a significant contingent of deeply devoted adherents who did not enter religious communities but instead struggled to find ways to combine contemplative spirituality with the demands of life "in the world."

The men (and a few women) who took to the deserts of Egypt, Palestine and Syria during the third to fifth centuries of the Christian era were on fire with zeal to give body and soul over to God. Drawing upon Hellenistic philosophy and practices as well as Jewish and Christian ones, they fashioned a way of life that often strikes people today as scandalously negative toward body, sexuality and secularity. Yet their more profound guiding ideals were compunction, purity of heart, hospitality and conversion by the Word of God. The severe discipline they exercised toward their own bodies was aimed at preparing those bodies to become radically transparent to God. The end for which asceticism was practiced was not destruction of the body, but rather clearing the way for the deification of the whole person. A story is told that when Abba Joseph was asked how one ought to pray, he spread out his hands to heaven and his fingers shone like ten candles; he said: "If you will, you could become a living flame."[1]

The desert monks were lay, that is, originally they had no special status or office setting them apart from other Christians, and they regarded their intense pursuit of God as nothing more than the full living of the Christian life. Even the few participants in the movement who were ordained were severely counseled that they must not expect any special conditions or treatment. Yet the desert movement clearly did separate its members from life "in the world" through geographical isolation, celibacy and intense ascetical practices. Within the social and economic conditions of the times these forms of separation served the purpose of freeing people from the claustrophobic demands of village life, in which every detail of one's existence was enmeshed in a web of customs and expectations that left little room for the kind of intimate confrontation with self and God that contemplation demands.[2] Lay adherents—many of them women—who could not literally go off to the desert still practiced a similar countercultural withdrawal within the confines of their own homes.

The institutionalization of the desert movement led into monasticism, for which this separation from ordinary secular life was a central dictum. The theology of seeking God primarily in the "earthly paradise" of the monastery, and ultimately in the heaven above the earth, flourished. Yet it is important to remember that the original impulse of these spiritualities was not elitist separation, but intense focus on living out the universal call to Christian discipleship.

Gradually, as monasticism became more firmly institutionalized and enwebbed in societal and ecclesial power structures, it became the norm for monks to be clerics—and for clerics to be called upon to live like monks. Religious life, originally a lay movement, became closely associated with the governing hierarchy of the Church, so that even today both male and female non-ordained members of religious communities are frequently seen as having a sort of middle status in between "clerical" and "lay."

A second key period for the development of Christian contemplative life took place during the eleventh to thirteenth centuries, when the ideal of the *vita apostolica* inspired tens of thousands of people to fervor in taking up a dedicated way of life. This apostolic life—the effort to practice a literal imitation of the poor, communal, faith-filled, servant life of the apostles—fueled both evangelical and eremitical aspirations; in the context of the times, these two were not seen as contradictory but as the two sides of the same coin. Among those who claimed an eremitical vocation during this period, many did not actually live a solitary life. Rather, they abandoned ordinary economic securities to live a relatively unconstrained life of availability for service, preaching and prayer among the poor.[3] Like the first desert contemplatives, these, too, were laity; they rejoiced in the poverty of being among the people without special status or protection.

The experiments of the *vita apostolica* engaged not only single people, but married couples with families as well. One of the largest movements of this sort was the *Humiliati* or "Humble Ones," in which families practiced prayer and mutual support and earned their living by clothmaking while they preached the gospel and served the poor. Originating among the laity of Lombardy, the *Humiliati* also developed branches for clergy and religious; by 1298 there were reported to be 389 religious houses and uncounted numbers of lay adherents.[4]

Since part of the ideal of the *vita apostolica* was communal living, it was not uncommon for those inspired by the eremitical and evangelical ideal to form small communities. The further institutionalization of some of these groups fed into the great religious communities that aspire to an eremitical spirituality—the Cistercians, Carmelites, Carthusians and Camaldolese. Even to this day these traditions nourish vast numbers of Christians from all walks of life who thirst for a contemplative spirituality.

The mendicant and apostolic forms of religious life also have their roots in this period. These groups dropped the confining structures of monastic cloister and constant liturgical prayer in favor of greater availability for service to the people of God. Once again many of the groups that eventually became religious communities originated with fervent laity seeking to intensify their Christian lives of prayer and service. Experiments with dedicated life apart from established religious communities proliferated, and religious life itself was no longer seen as necessarily requiring the geographical segregation emphasized by monasticism. Other forms of separation—the habit, celibacy, highly structured rules of life—more often than not remained, however.

These movements—the wandering hermits, the *Humiliati*, the mendicants and other new experiments—that grew out of the *vita apostolica* spirituality facilitated a significant, although still partial, shift toward dedicated Christian life combined with presence and participation in the secular world.

■ WHAT IS 'NEW' ABOUT LAY CONTEMPLATION?

It may be that today's lay contemplative movement represents the early spring buds of a third great flowering of dedicated Christian life—one that, this time, may complete the trajectory toward contemplative engagement in every dimension of human life. To appreciate this radical shift, we need to understand the way contemplation and action have been understood theologically in the past.

At the risk of oversimplification, we can say that from its origins in the patristic era until relatively recently, classical Christian theology and spirituality have been deeply shaped by a symbolic and conceptual worldview that envisions divine realities as "descending" from a transcendent spiritual realm into the material realm, while human spirituality is seen as having to do with "ascending" from the material to the spiritual realm. Although this worldview is often called "dualistic," in the strict sense it is not—since both spiritual and material realms have their source and goal in the single transcendent dimension. Nevertheless, it clearly sets up a hierarchy in which physical, secular, worldly realities are less intrinsically close to God than are spiritual, sacred, religious realities.

The consequence of this classical Christian theology was a spirituality in which those who are most serious about knowing and loving God are those who can dissociate themselves from "worldly" sexual, economic and political life in favor of full-time dedication to explicitly religious activities. As long as this theology and spirituality prevailed, it was inevitable that the Christian life of those wholly engaged in the secular world would be devalued in relation to that of the hierarchically superior church leaders and a closely associated separate category of those living a "religious" life.

Throughout the patristic and medieval eras, a positive dimension of this classical synthesis was that it placed contemplation at the center of ecclesial life. The shadow side, however, was that it marginalized the majority of Christian laity in favor of an honored elite who could associate themselves with this favored contemplative center through ordination or religious vows. As the modern era began to dawn in the sixteenth and seventeenth centuries, a significant cultural and ideological shift took place. Human capacities for reason and the domination of the physical world moved into a much more prominent place at the top of the hierarchical pyramid. Contemplation began to be viewed as a marginal and largely extraneous endeavor, closely associated with irrationality and the "merely" emotional.

As the theological justification for hierarchical structures in the Church largely lost its contemplative center, these structures became rationalized and hardened. The result of all this was a Church centered on its clergy, with both the laity *and* the contemplative life on the margins. The move into modernity, in short, took the vital contemplative core out of the classical hierarchical understanding of Christian life, and yet left the basic structure standing.

The glory and the pain of Christian theology today is that this interim synthesis is in the midst of breaking down, to be replaced by what may appear to many as a cacophony of disparate voices. Emerging in this cacophony is a very different and non-hierarchical way of envisioning humanity in relation to God and the world. It is a vision of spirit-in-the-world instead of spirit-against-the-world; it emphasizes God as an active force of transformation in every dimension of creation instead of God as calling the elect forth from the entanglements of creation. It is only in view of this shift in theology that we begin to glimpse the fresh meaning of the term *contemplative* as it is coming to birth in the world today. The lay contemplative movement is, at least potentially, an embodiment of a spirituality of God radically manifest in the midst of everyday, secular life. The essays in this volume offer a variety of glimpses into that emerging vision.

■ NOTES

[1] "Sayings of the Desert Fathers," 12,8, in Owen Chadwick, ed., *Western Asceticism* (Philadelphia: Westminster, 1958).

[2] See, for example, Peter Brown, *The Making of Late Antiquity* (Cambridge, Mass.: Harvard University Press, 1978); or Margaret Miles, *Practicing Christianity: Critical Perspectives for an Embodied Spirituality* (New York: Crossroad, 1990).

[3] Henrietta Leyser, *Hermits and the New Monasticism: A Study of Religious Communities in Western Europe, 1000-1150* (New York: St. Martin's Press, 1984).

[4] Cf. Lester K. Little, *Religious Poverty and the Profit Economy in Medieval Europe* (Ithaca, N.Y.: Cornell University Press, 1983), pp. 113-20.

PART ONE

THE LAY CONTEMPLATIVE EXPERIENCE

Introduction to the Testimonies

by Deborah A. Gephardt

For the lay contemplative living at the turn of the twentieth century, the attempt to orient one's life decisions in obedience to a dimension deemed invisible or even nonexistent by society's standards, is a daunting and courageous task. Learning to choose less instead of more, emptiness instead of accomplishments, simplicity and natural harmony instead of cutting edge—these constant choices appear in learning the art of contemplative living. How is the contemplative today, often severed from institutional support, to be guided, nurtured into ever deeper awareness and unity? Where does one get advice to develop a sense of resonance and harmony about one's vision, about the twists and turns on the journey? Nourishment and support are necessary for a sense of balance and humor, for courage and perseverance in this new way of living and embracing the universe.

Theology, ideas and concepts are all of great help at some stages of the journey. They can entice, open new vistas and broaden horizons, allowing one to test, weigh and choose, making the unknown terrain somewhat more comfortable and familiar.

Yet one becomes aware eventually that ideas and concepts are like menus, and, like menus, cannot suffice for nourishment. Ultimately it is experience, life itself, that is the Sacred Teacher. Where, before, concepts illuminated and fed the soul, now nothing becomes more nourishing than learning the lessons of life and connecting with others on this spiritual path. One's own personal circumstances and choices in this locus of time and space are now seen as a sacred microcosmic unfolding of life itself. Concepts become as shadows compared to how others and I live life in this sacred moment.

11

In the history of the contemplative journey stories of personal experience have held a cherished and honored place. In all religious traditions wisdom stories emerge from the fruits of contemplation— insights from others constantly learning this art of contemplative living.

For the lay contemplative, the paradox of recognized oneness with the universe along with the often simultaneous feeling of aloneness in the ordinary societal sense brings a longing to integrate this and other paradoxes into one's life. Stories can nourish that integration and offer sustenance.

We may read or hear stories that tell us where we have been. In this way we say, "Yes, I am in communion with you in this experience." We also need those stories that show us where we have not yet gone to beckon us onward, to indicate new landscape, to let the owner's experiences speak their communion within us. These stories leap like life-giving sparks back and forth from one heart and soul to another, uniting and kindling us through time and space. It matters not whether one's soul companions are ancient spiritual mothers and fathers, canonized saints or neighbors. That they articulate our tremblings and our vision is enough.

Among the authors of the stories that follow, some are married, some single, some are religious, some former religious or monks. All are living in their own unique ways in the external world of change their steadfast and unchanging response to an inward contemplative call. In and through their unfoldings, we resonate and feel anew that wondrous tug of the Divine that draws us ever deeper into its orbit. We are refreshed and renewed in our own deepest harmony by their sharing. We are grateful for their lives among us.

CHAPTER ONE

Contemplation: Journey Inward or Journey Outward?

by Robert Durback

My entry into the deeper levels of contemplative prayer began on the day I lost everything. It was February 10, 1964. Standing alone in a room in the infirmary at Gethsemani Abbey in Kentucky, burned out and broken physically and psychologically, I had made the dreaded decision which could no longer be put off. With the help of my good friend and guide, John Eudes Bamberger, a monk/psychiatrist at the abbey, I decided to leave the monastery.

On the bed in front of me were a pair of black pants, a matching suit jacket, a belt, a shirt and a dark, heavy overcoat. My task was to remove what I was wearing and put on the clothes spread out before me. I cringed at the idea. Changing into these clothes I hadn't worn for years posed a threat to me, a reversal that disturbed me deeply. It meant a demotion, being stripped of my identity, giving up who I was, to become who I was not yet.

The only identity I had known for the past thirteen years was symbolized in the clothes I was wearing as I stood looking at the clothes thrown across the bed before me. My white robe and black scapular, firmed around my waist by a leather belt, made me aware that I was a Trappist monk bound by solemn vows to live as a monk until death. I had been wearing this distinctive garb during the most formative years in my life, from the age of eighteen in 1950, to this cold winter morning in February of 1964.

Yes, I had heard it said many times that the habit does not make the monk. But the habit did remind me of what I was supposed to be, what I wanted to be: a man of prayer, a man for whom God was to be the All in All of my life. Now I had reached the point of having to give up all that; not my deepest desires, which flared up in me now with an even greater intensity, but the protective framework that guarded and fed that flame. That was the hard part. It was the first time in my life that I had prayed for days that I might die rather than have to face this moment of separation, this divorce. But people were waiting for me. There was no time to die. I had to catch a plane I didn't want to catch.

The focus of this book revolves around the question, "How do lay people live the contemplative life outside the fixed boundaries of traditional, institutionalized religious life?"

Before attempting to answer the question as posed, I'd like to clarify my own understanding of what is meant by "the contemplative life." In monastic circles these words are part of an accepted vocabulary. The presumption is that there is at least some basic common understanding of their meaning. I remember getting my first jolt from my presuppositions one afternoon while still in the monastery, reading an article by Thomas Merton. A single sentence jumped off the page: "Anyone who hasn't meditated on Auschwitz doesn't know anything about meditation." It was like I had just finished arranging the furniture in my living room to the ultimate in artistry and design and suddenly a bulldozer came ploughing through the front door to reduce it all to rubble.

I think Merton would approve if I were to edit his statement to read: "Anyone who hasn't contemplated Auschwitz doesn't know anything about contemplation." Contemplation is not about escaping to some celestial dream world that offers immunization from concern with the evils in the world around us. The first meaning given to the word *contemplate* in Webster is: "to view or consider with continued attention." It means *fixed attention* for one thing. Scanning the newspaper is not contemplation, until one item catches my attention and I stop scanning and start "contemplating." When I *contemplate* I allow what I read or see or hear to *touch me*.

In those first weeks and months outside the monastery, outside "the contemplative life," high on my list of priorities was the determination to pursue every means available to me that would help me integrate into my new situation the good habits I had learned in the monastery: securing a place for myself that would guarantee a measure of silence and solitude—a place where I could give my *fixed attention* to the deeper Presence in my life. With the kind help of my brother-in-law I was able to fix up a room in my mother's basement that would provide me with that sacred space where I could read, pray and reflect alone and in silence, and so keep myself available and attentive to the voice of God.

Ironically, the breakthrough came not when I was absorbed in the "holy" in my basement hideaway. It came late one afternoon ten months after I had left the monastery when I picked up the daily newspaper, intending to browse. The story on the front page instantly grabbed my attention.

The headline read: **TEENAGE GIRL FOUND SLAIN IN HOME.** Every violent death is shocking. But the savagery of this one sent tremors rocking the whole community.

It was three days after Christmas. Beverly was enjoying the holidays, having lunch with her grandmother. She left shortly after lunch, as she had arranged to meet her girlfriend at 1:15 that afternoon. Her grandmother's neighbor drove her home, watched her go in the front door and drove away.

Her girlfriend arrived promptly at 1:15, rang the doorbell, but got no answer. The door was locked. She lingered, hoping Beverly would eventually show up. Hearing a blaring radio inside, she thought it uncharacteristic of Beverly to play music so loudly and ignore her friend standing outside. At about 1:25 she heard a thud coming from the upstairs like heavy furniture hitting the floor.

Annoyance turned to concern. Something was wrong. She decided to call Beverly's grandmother. Alarmed, Beverly's grandmother immediately called Beverly's mother at work. The mother promptly called the father, who worked closer to home. The father raced home, unlocked the front door, ran upstairs and found a grisly sight: his sixteen-year-old daughter lying on the bedroom floor in a pool of blood. Blood all over the walls. Beverly had been strangled and stabbed forty times. Her mother, who by this time was on her way to the house, was met by a neighbor who informed her bluntly: "Beverly has been stabbed to death."

I did not scan this story. I contemplated it. As I read the harrowing details, I thought to myself, "You think you have troubles. Can you imagine the trauma this family is going through!" The psychological burden of loss I had been carrying receded as Beverly's story moved to the center of my attention.

Contemplation at a given point moves from "fixed attention" to *identification*. One *becomes one with* the object one is contemplating. Beverly and her parents were no longer separate from me. Their pain became my pain. I could not be a bystander. I felt deeply the need to share the family's grief. I had no car. But there were buses. I decided to go to the wake.

I walked into the funeral parlor a total stranger. I had never done this before. But I *knew* the family with my heart. And they received me into their hearts. After I had shared a little of my own story with them, they asked that I say a few words to Beverly's twelve-year-old sister and to her grandmother and grandfather. I came to comfort and left being the one comforted by being received so warmly, stranger though I was.

Contemplation begins with *fixed attention* and moves to *identification*. Identification seeks a further dimension: *communion*. After the funeral I began writing to the family, asking at the start for a picture of Beverly. The picture was sent, with details about Beverly's interests and achievements in school. The exchanges continued. Eventually a letter came inviting me to come for evening dinner with the family in their home. I was deeply touched by the invitation. What a grace to sit at table and break bread with this grief-stricken family, and even to be able to evoke some laughter. I was shown the poetry Beverly had written and saw at once what a gifted child she was. Her physical beauty and giftedness only added more to the enigma of the manner of her death.

It should come as no surprise that I cannot end this story by saying that the family in question "lived happily ever after." The killer was never found. The parents announced their divorce some years later, almost a statistical given in the case of parents who have lost a child. Still, in this case, they remain friends. Neither has remarried. They live apart but keep in touch. By now they are in their early seventies.

Every year for the past thirty-three years I have called the mother on December 28, the anniversary date of Beverly's death. Some years she beats me to the phone. If I'm out of town, I call her from wherever I am. Her Christmas card shines brightly in my holiday mail.

But what has all this got to do with contemplation? I can only answer that there are different ways of living or speaking about the contemplative life. There is much to be gained from studies about prayer. But having been engaged in such study for a good portion of my life, I must conclude with my many mentors that all prayer ultimately has to be integrated with life—not somebody else's life, my life, the who and where I am right now. I like what Robert C. Morris wrote not long ago in *Weavings*:

> Scripture is bolder than our piety. Restricting our imagery to the conventional hinders people from claiming God's presence when their lives lead them into some strange land.
>
> If I look for my familiar Shepherd God at the moment when I am facing the Whirlwind (see Job 38:1), I may conclude there is no God there. Spontaneous images of God, especially those that come in response to our honest question, How are you here?, are often the unveiling of a Face that will change not only the relationship, but us.[1]

My experience tells me that the contemplative life is not lived in the head, nor does it originate in the head. It is a stream that flows out from the heart of the crucified and risen Jesus. It is a stream that flows into barren desert places thirsting for life, a stream that seeks out what is broken, discarded, given up as dead. The contemplative life is not the luxury of a spiritual elite who dine daily on wine and caviar. It is the life of those who thirst for the stream of living water. It is the life of those who follow the stream to hidden, barren, desolate places.

That stream reached me at a time when I was parched with thirst. It was channeled to me through a family whose desolation and desperation was greater than mine. In reaching out to them in my own wounded condition, I was healed. When I was with this family I knew I was standing on holy ground, for "The Lord is near to the brokenhearted; and saves the crushed in spirit" (Psalm 34).

Before I left Gethsemani, once I had made the decision to leave, I approached Thomas Merton, who was novice master at the time, and asked if I could see him for a few minutes. I had informed him that I would soon be leaving. He made me a sign that he was "up to his neck in work," but would see if he could squeeze me in somehow. Later in the day he passed me a note saying he would see me at the first bell for Mass on Sunday morning, the next day.

Those were precious moments. In the course of our discussion I asked if he would give me in writing a "sentence" I could take with me, something like the disciples of the desert fathers would ask of their "abbas" from time to time. He promised he would. Typically, he gave me much more than that, including his latest book, autographed. Later in the day he walked over to me as we were filing in for the evening meal and with a smile handed me a card with the "sentence" on it in his own handwriting. Here is what the card read:

God manifests himself in what is hidden. Therefore if you try to find Him you don't. He shows Himself when there is no "you" to look for Him. But whether He shows Himself or not does not matter because everything is a blessing from Him.

All the best. Stay close to Our Lady.

(Signed) Thomas Merton

I had the card framed. It hangs over my desk to this day as I write this. It's my compass.

Somehow I can't help but see a bit of irony, even humor, in that one sentence: "He shows himself when there is no 'you' to look for Him." My mind travels to that runaway monk in the upper room of the monastery on that cold winter day in February some thirty-three years ago, fretting about "losing" himself.

■ NOTES

[1] *Weavings*, January-February 1997, p. 30.

CHAPTER TWO

Contemplative Living in Ordinary Time

by Barbara E. Scott

It's Saturday afternoon and I'm the on-call chaplain at a local hospital. It's been a busy day. I responded to several calls; distributed Communion to the Catholic patients; followed up on patients I had seen yesterday; then sat, with aching feet, in the hospital chapel. I am too weary to make the Stations of the Cross as I had done the previous night, bringing the burdens of patients and their families to Jesus. I simply sit before the eucharistic presence, allowing the people in my heart to spill out and fill the tiny sanctuary.

There is John, in his late eighties, unable to hear me unless I shout, who asked if I would "pull up a chair, please" while he recited his litany of gratitude to his Creator. There is Martin, forty-eight, who has battled brain cancer for six years. In these last days of his life Martin was brought to the hospital to receive medication for his constant seizures. With Martin are his wife and grown daughter. They appear to me as two fair-haired angels at Martin's side, each holding one of Martin's hands, each stroking his hand with tenderness, each speaking words of love and comfort while Martin endures yet another seizure. There is young Sue, married just five months, who survived a car accident that killed her husband. There is Emma, ninety-four years young, who can't wait to receive Jesus in Communion and wonders if I have time to hear "all" her prayers. There is Mike who died in the emergency room. I am waiting for his family; they live three hours away.

The chapel is filled with these people. These are your people, Jesus. I bring them to you. Give them your healing love and peace. I allow Jesus to heal me, to minister to me. "Be still, Barbara. You are mine. I will refresh you. I will restore your strength like the eagle's."

And then there are no words, only a presence.

Although I only work a few days a month as a hospital chaplain, this ministry is a major part of my contemplative journey. Being on call is my contemplative fasting. Fasting from my own plans and desires, I am available to the needs of others. I am open and ready for the unknown. I surrender to the "I know not what." I respond to others' needs, not out of my strength and knowledge, but out of my nothingness. I become nothing so that Christ can become all. Surrendering, allowing, opening, listening, setting myself aside to let other people and their needs occupy my heart; trusting, waiting, feeling my inadequacies before so much pain and suffering. Figuratively, I am always taking my shoes off. I am always on holy ground. The Divine is close to the brokenhearted. And I am called to share this ground. Each person I am called to be with, to remain with on this holy ground, becomes my teacher.

My contemplative abstinence comes from my work as a spiritual director. Spiritual direction requires me to abstain from my own insights, thoughts and ideas, to listen, really listen, with the directee to the Spirit working in the directee's life. I am only a guide. The real drama in spiritual direction is between the Spirit and the directee. I abstain. I set myself aside and wait upon others to disclose themselves to me until they have reached the place of greater self-awareness, self-understanding, self-acceptance and self-love that enables them to move deeper into the Divine. The people who have asked me to be their spiritual guide have blessed me with their requests, their trust, their self-disclosures. These, too, are my teachers.

I have two contemplative communities. The larger one is the Association of Contemplative Sisters, of which I have been a member almost from its beginnings in 1969. In this sisterhood I have found some of my dearest and deepest friendships. In ACS I have been affirmed, loved, accepted, challenged and transformed. I need my contemplative sisters to mirror and model for me their unique contemplative life-styles. In this sisterhood I have prayed and played, sung and danced, laughed and cried, shared deeply and sat in silence.

I have served ACS in regional leadership roles for ten years. In 1996 I was a candidate for national ACS president. Minutes before the discernment process that would decide who would be the next president, I felt misgivings well up inside of me: Someone else could do the work. I tasted, in some small way, Christ's bitterness in the Agony in the Garden, "If it is possible, let this cup pass from me." Then a member of the ACS came up to me and said, "I can't imagine anyone being president...except you." Her comment startled me. Was she an angel sent into my garden? The misgivings dissipated. "Thy will be done." If I was elected I would embrace the office wholeheartedly. If not, fine. Through the whole discernment process I was at peace. My ego was sitting like a "weaned child with its mother" (Psalm 131:2). Several months into the office, I realized why I had misgivings. The office of president was not for my glory, but for my growth. Being ACS president would transform me—has transformed me.

My other contemplative community is quite small, comprised of two humans, Sue and I, and three cats, Bo, Fro and LadyBug. Sue and I have lived and grown together for the past twenty-four years. We have quite different personalities. This difference has provided fuel for comfort and confrontation, compassion and challenge, for life-giving sharing, praying and companioning one another in our contemplative journeys.

Our home—a log house in the woods on a lake—is a dream fulfilled. The woods are home to a multitude of forest dwellers. In winter I ski and walk on the lake. In spring, summer, fall, I canoe the lake, venturing out in the early morning fog to await sunrise.

In the morning light I have watched kingfishers diving and blue heron stalking the shoreline for breakfast. I have watched red-winged black birds guard their nests among the cattails; seen turtles of all sizes crawl out of the lake onto rocks and logs to sun themselves; witnessed loons teach their young to dive for fish. In the multicolored hues of sunset I have experienced dragonflies feasting on mosquitoes that hum around me. I have observed a mother duck leading her newborn chicks around the tall, safe grasses.

I have been surprised by beaver slapping their tails on the water to protest my presence, the shotgun-like sound startling the deer that have come down to the lake to drink. I have learned to feel the drumming of grouse on a hollow log. I know how to remain absolutely still while a family of bear ambles toward a blueberry marsh. I have frightened numerous waterfowl and caused otter to slip into the water as I slowly made my way through the narrow half-mile tributary that leads to another lake.

I know where to find the bright yellow marsh marigolds covering swampy ground. I know where to discover blood root, trillium, Indian pipe and every kind of wildflower that grows in these woods. I have found blackberries and raspberries and know how to pick my share, leaving the rest for the forest dwellers. Night is special anytime of year. I have counted falling stars, traced the Milky Way, been surprised by a bolide, heard a meteor sizzle overhead and stared at dancing Northern Lights until I thought my neck would break from looking up so long.

These woods call me, again and again, to take my shoes off, for here, too, I am on sacred ground. Nature is my daily contemplative guide revealing to me the splendor hidden within my ordinary time.

CHAPTER THREE

The Call to Life 'on the Margins'

by Kathryn Damiano

Perhaps my call to the contemplative life began with a predisposi-tion toward silence and solitude that was fostered during my early formative years by the privilege of having the upstairs of my child-hood home all to myself. This space consisted of a bedroom, a den and a half bath. It was there I learned to enjoy my own companion-ship and to spend many hours in friendship with silence.

This environment, I believe, nourished my natural inclination to trust my own spiritual experience. Because of this reliance on inner spiritual authority, I can retrospectively say that God gave me the makings to be a Quaker. I didn't come to realize this formally until later in my life.

As I have reflected on my contemplative calling, I recognize three core themes running through it. The first theme is *liminality*. When I came across this term, which is traditionally used by anthropologists and more recently by monastic orders, it was a sanity check. I found that God does create across cultures in every generation those who symbolically embody standing on the threshold between what is and what is yet to come.

As a woman who entered seminary in the mid-1970's when fewer than a quarter of the student population was female, I was downright liminal. These were times when excessive use of "He," "Father" and "brethren" was opposed by the women seminarians (and a few men) standing and blowing whistles. As I pursued my studies, I was radi-calized even further. As you might imagine, I had serious trouble adopting Jesus as my model for salvation in this environment. I struggled with the concept of a male savior who was to exemplify wholeness for women. I also felt in the depths of my being that it was idolatrous to worship Jesus while forsaking his admonition to realize the kingdom/community of God right here and now.

Being liminal was my way "into" Jesus. As I was "heard into Being" by other students and some teachers, I recognized that my call was to remain on the margin of the institutional Church. Then I "discovered" that this was the call of Jesus, too! I identified with Jesus not as an external model but as someone in whose life I participated. As a consequence, a spiritual power was brought forth in me that transformed my life as the life of Christ was inwardly replayed.

My perplexity continued as I questioned how the passion of Christ could be equated with the three hours on the cross. I had read stories of contemporary women being tortured in South American coups that could more than rival the crucifixion account. From the reality of my own truth, I recognized that the enduring passion of Christ is in the everyday experiences of injustice, humiliation and the folly of the human condition. This is a passion that does not always result in physical pain, but it engenders a pain that is suffered in hiddenness alone with God.

In this United Methodist Seminary (I was never Methodist but went there to study with a particular feminist theologian) I was influenced by a fellow student who was doing his field placement in a Friends organization. As I became more open to God's transforming work, I began to slip away on Sunday mornings to the nearest Quaker Meeting, which was about an hour away. It was among Friends that I found a spiritual home. This was a church that seemed to profess an experience of spiritual conversion that mirrored mine. Becoming a Friend meant not being ordained and therefore surrendering a means of livelihood. (Friends do not have professional clergy or laity. We are all potential ministers.) As a liminal person, I live into the in-between times that encompass the longing, the waiting and the unconsummated desire. I am driven to prayer, and to be sustained I must rely on Divine Providence.

The second theme of my contemplative call is *confronting the principalities and powers*. There is a freedom and a confidence that accompany a contemplative life. One is less controlled by the usual ambition, desire for money and things, need for approval or being bought off for power. Though I witness to the fact that "my kingdom is not of this world," those in worldly power seem to be particularly threatened. I have come smack up against the limitations of human relationships and human justice. As a consequence, I experience the sacrament of failure and am even tempted to despair.

There has been a movement in my prayer over the years as I continue to encounter the principalities and powers that are especially rampant in today's institutions. My "God fix this!" prayer has often been confounded when there are no visible results. I have stayed in a variety of these oppressive situations almost beyond tolerance. Yet as I persevered, I have been graced with little redemptions that I take as indications that God has not finished using me as an instrument. In fact, the message was to radiate the love of Christ.

As I have explored the range of understandings about power and Church governance, I have come to see that Jesus' life was a testimony to an alternative concept of power. He was tempted by the same economic, political and religious demons that I had experienced. Jesus broke the cycle of violence and responded instead with love. He remained hidden for most of his life, healed relatively few and finally aroused so much opposition that he was put to death.

I remember seeing a *Twilight Zone* episode years ago in which a certain culture had "sin eaters." Their function was to bear the burdens of others. Was I being asked to bear the burdens of institutions as part of a redemptive process? In these broken institutions, I could sense a movement in progress on a cosmic level. I did not fully understand the process, but sensed I was called to cooperate with it. When I am released from this use in God's time, I fall back into financial insecurity. Yet I am also deeply blessed with times of "enkindling," a respite that is infused with God's undergirding love.

The third theme of my contemplative path, *eschatology*, flows directly from the others. My flavor of contemplative seems to be called to demonstrate that in this broken world not all healing comes through human hands. The solitary person lives a life of "relevant irrelevancy." I am asked to trust God in situations that seem to oppose God. Prayer becomes a revolutionary act in defiance of what is, in the promise that God will liberate. I become more and more convinced of "things not seen." I begin to subject life to the criterion of eternity.

I have learned much about eschatology in caring for elderly people. Many are natural contemplatives. The fullness of their lives is contagious. My most recent experience has been in caring for retired nuns, some of whom were semicomatose or cognitively impaired. I would "wire the sisters for sound" with a Walkman playing healing Gregorian chants. My response was a ministry of presence to the life essence that remained in these sisters. I could commune with their energy through the practice of therapeutic touch. The redemptive suffering of these sisters elicited love from me. I was the one being redeemed!

On other occasions when a sister's dying was imminent, staff and residents were often invited to sing and pray her into paradise. What touched me most deeply was the tangibility of the eternal. Heaven was so real that it was as if the dying sister was moving to Pittsburgh and we would all be with her soon. The contemplative person dips into the eschatological and discovers things as they really are and enjoys them to the fullest.

As I enter another chapter of my life, I discern the quickenings of the Holy Spirit. God remains so inside me that God cannot be analyzed from the outside. What will God call forth from me next? Throughout Christian history, there have been those called to a life of solitude and prayer—particularly in times of Church renewal. I know I am to be part of that movement, but the form is still opaque. I continue to show up in faithfulness.

CHAPTER FOUR

Together on the Contemplative Journey

by Ruth and Mark Dundon

As we were wondering what we might share that would be of interest to others, some of our friends commented, "You don't seem to realize how extraordinary it is for a couple to be *together* on the spiritual path in this day and age!" This was enough to give us the courage to share what we have come to believe is the most important, enduring and stabilizing part of our marriage and life, namely, our shared contemplative journeys.

We started out our journeys in different places and times. Mark grew up as the youngest of three in a Catholic family in the Upper Peninsula of Michigan. Religion was an important part of the family experience. It wasn't until he got to St. John's University in Collegeville, Minnesota, that a deeper sense of spirituality started to take root. The wonderful Benedictine practice of Liturgy of the Hours and Eucharist created a lasting impression. His favorite service was Compline, said in the dormitory each evening, and Psalm 91 is deeply planted to this day.

Ruth started her journey as the middle of nine children raised on a farm near New Munich, Minnesota. The church was the center of this German Catholic rural community, and Ruth was spiritually alive from an early age. The Franciscan spirituality she encountered while attending St. Francis High School in Little Falls, Minnesota, made a very deep impression. She became a nurse after high school, trained by the Benedictine Sisters in St. Cloud, and was actively involved in the Sodality.

We met while Ruth was in nurses' training and Mark was working as an orderly at the St. Cloud Hospital while in college. After Mark completed his military service we were married and Mark went to graduate school. Children were part of our early married lives and an important part of our spiritual growth. From the start both of us were actively involved in many faith-building activities. The contemplative side of our growth really began, however, with transcendental meditation, which created a thirst for a Christian form of meditation.

Our prayers were answered when we moved to Leavenworth, Kansas, and met Father Edward Hays at Shantivanam in Easton, Kansas. Father Ed launched us on a powerful journey that continues to evolve. We started the practice of two prayer periods a day in 1979. Since then we have continued to learn about meditation through reading, personal experience and guidance from Father Ed, Jennifer Sullivan and the staff at Shantivanam.

When we moved to Bellevue, Washington, in the mid-1980's, Ruth took a twenty-four-week course in Centering Prayer with Father Thomas Keating. She eventually began facilitating the series for a retreat center. It was a wonderful, growthful experience. In 1991 she took formation training through Contemplative Outreach, the organization Father Keating started. This helped to deepen her prayer life and her understanding of the conceptual background of the spiritual journey and contemplative life.

In 1992 we moved to Kentucky, and Ruth was asked to be the area coordinator for Contemplative Outreach. There is a thirst for this form of prayer, and in these last few years many groups have learned the practice of Centering Prayer. Being privileged to share so many people's stories and their personal growth through the discipline of Centering Prayer, the continued support of small groups and the Contemplative Outreach programs has been a tremendous help in our journey. Because of these experiences, we have remained faithful to the discipline and gained new insight into the ways God works in the lives of others. That, in turn, helps us to see how God is doing the same things in our own lives.

Our personal commitment to Centering Prayer has grown through the years. Although Mark went through the first series of tapes several times, it was Ruth who taught Mark the essentials of this way of praying. We both have gone to intensive Centering Prayer retreats, and we have found them to be powerful and helpful in deepening our commitment, our understanding and our relationship to God and each other.

We are tremendously different from one another, but what we share most deeply is a common commitment to prayer and spiritual growth. Mark's job has required a lot of traveling so we are separated a lot; our prayer helps us feel connected. We feel a shared presence whether we are together or separated. Our commitment has also been a great help to Mark in the constant struggle of getting in a second prayer time with his busy work and travel schedule.

Right now we are in the midst of one of the most challenging transitions of our life together, especially for Mark as he faces an early and unplanned retirement. It is a shock to think that after all the years of work there will be no more. In a sense Mark is at the prime of his career as a CEO. He is being merged out of his position because the new organization wants a change at the top. So far, things are going pretty well, as we are able to process our feelings together, supporting, reflecting and affirming each other as we go along. There is no blaming, and he continues to hold a steady course for the organization and the people working for him.

Mark says the two key things that keep this from getting the best of him are his relationship with Ruth—a healthy one of more than thirty-five years—and his relationship with God. Centering Prayer has helped him understand that there is more to life than a job and that there is plenty of personal work to be done. We have a strong belief that God is a part of this, that God is faithful and that this situation can be a growth experience for us both. We are being given practice in letting go as we are shown where the false self is still active and where there are areas in our lives that are unhealed. Centering Prayer has given us tools to deal with—even to welcome, embrace and integrate—difficult situations and to be grateful for everything.

Centering Prayer has given us insight that helps us deal more effectively with all the issues we face in everyday life. As we have come to a deeper awareness of God's activity in our everyday life, our work, children and each other, we have begun to take more personal responsibility for our feelings and actions. One of the most important things we have learned is to see our feelings as a sign of our values. It was disheartening at first to see our self-centered motivations and values. Now, however, we realize how freeing it has become not to be controlled by our emotions and to be more capable of choosing our responses. We can accept each other's faults better as we have become less defensive and realize that by working together we can process our issues more effectively.

We have three children, all grown adults. They are all aware of Centering Prayer and have good memories of their experiences with meditation at Shantivanam when they were young. From the time they were children we have told them to remember that they have a spirit and to find ways to nourish it. We knew they would do it in different ways than we did. It turns out that they are all interested in spiritual growth and practice some form of meditation.

It has been helpful for them to see that we are working on our issues as a normal part of growth on the spiritual journey. We get help if we need it, and we share our experiences with them as we go along. Our personal growth commitments have encouraged the children to deal with their own issues, which is most gratifying to us. We also are not so judgmental about the ways they behave. We know they have to learn about who they are and deal in their own way with the residue of difficult experiences from their early years, just as we have had to do.

One of our most painful, but also growth-producing experiences occurred several years ago when Ruth's brother died of AIDS. Ruth remembers when he told her of his HIV status, which was a death sentence in those days. At that time she promised to be there for him no matter what happened. With the full support of Mark and the children, it was possible to fulfill that promise. Being with him in his struggles was both a challenge and an opportunity to love and support him in a way he never thought possible. Ruth was the only one in his family who knew he was gay and that he had been counseled out of the seminary because of that fact, leaving him feeling rejected and unlovable. The practice of Centering Prayer taught Ruth that regardless of the ups and downs he experienced and the anger he projected on her as he worked through his feelings and made his peace, she could flow with it and keep her focus on caring for, supporting and loving him unconditionally.

Ruth and our two daughters were with him when he died. Sharing that experience was a great blessing. As they sang to him, "I will never forget you, I will never forsake you," our daughter Jackie, in tears, turned to her sister and said, "Mary, Mom will never forsake us." The support of our two daughters while he was dying and, after he died, of our son Dan, brought us closer together. This experience showed all of us how essential it is to ground our lives in prayer.

Although it was a time of great stress, much travel and time apart, we were able to stay focused and centered on God's love and to respond to the Spirit's prompting. This provided the strength, courage and patience to support each other and to care lovingly for

Ruth's brother, in spite of the social stigma, prejudice and fear surrounding his illness. We believe that the many years of the practice of letting go through Centering Prayer prepared us for letting one of our loved ones go. We trust that now our precious brother is in a place where he knows he is loved just as he is.

When we married we said yes to being sacrament to each other, to manifest God's love to each other in good and bad times, in sickness and health, "until death do us part." That is our commitment to each other, and with God's grace and love we know even more clearly today that it is possible to keep. Contemplative practice in the form of Centering Prayer has been very much a part of this journey. It has helped us to be aware of God's presence each day, in the surprises, the joys and sorrows, and especially in the ordinary.

CHAPTER FIVE

God in Flesh and Spirit

by Ann G. Denham

Finding contemplation was a homecoming that loosed chaos in my life. Nothing in my Methodist tradition had prepared me for the forces released by intensive prayer and meditation. Expecting some cozy chats with the Lord, I was thrust into light and a landscape out of Vincent Van Gogh; a strong visual sense of a multilayered reality and a howling fear-storm straight from a dank, black hole.

In desperation I flew from my home in California to the East Coast to consult Elizabeth, a religious of the Cenacle whom I trusted. She offered assurance that I was not lost. She said my experience was classic and added: "Most people doing such intensive work are in a convent or an ashram." Dropping me at the airport, she advised: "When you get home, watch and see what is given back to you." I boarded the plane with two burning questions: How would I live "without skin," and what would become of my marriage?

Much would not be returned: my ordination; my doctoral program and hopes for seminary teaching; my secret hunch that I was going to be a saint. But against all writings I could discover, my marriage would be given back in a tumultuous gift of love and my husband, non-religious, without metaphor or path, would shelter me until I learned to bear the light.

The contemplative journey is described in various religious writings. There is a time of purification or stripping away of attachments; a time of illumination, when the soul receives graces and communications from God; a time of union, when the soul is united with the Divine. John of the Cross writes of nights; Teresa of Avila talks about chambers. Other authors elaborate, but I could not locate my experiences in this progression. I was inclined to think this was because I was married. I did feel like a bride, wooed and chosen, but I also worried about being drawn away from my husband and my marriage.

Ours was a growing, evolving marriage of twenty-six years. Two questing persons on separate paths, we shared history and space, loving the life we had created, relieved that our daughter and two sons were grown. Now, we had a time and place for us. Walter was immersed in reform of mathematics education, in California and beyond. In our son's emptied room, with an altar made of a laundry hamper, I was, depending upon interpretation, playing convent or learning to pray. That God would answer my stumbling communication blew my mind.

I had thought it would probably be hard to find time and space to meditate, busy as I was being a wife, housewife, mother and grandmother. I didn't realize I would be forced to reinvent my life, based on the proposition that marriage can be a locus for the contemplative journey.

Everything I read said it couldn't be done. Every married mystic I tracked down was first a widow or had made the "brother and sister vow." It seemed to be taken for granted that sexual energies would be sublimated to aid in entering deeper into the Mystery. Other writers took a dimmer view. Sexual feelings were temptation, barrier, sin. And what of the basic but far from trivial situation of stripping away my defenses and my habits at the same time I was driving the freeway, caring for babies and being Mrs. Walter Denham? I looked in vain for a book, my solution to everything, that would spell out what was right and wrong.

God kept wooing, light and desire and longing; prayer that wrapped me round and sweetness I could taste on my tongue. There were mornings cold and gray, when an icy fear enveloped me and I couldn't find my way downstairs, much less to the supermarket to shop for dinner. I dreamed of a hermitage, of solitude, and we talked of just such a possibility. For a man unversed in the shape of the contemplative journey, Walter was tender and quick to suggest ways and means.

He never once complained that he had a mad woman on his hands. On the road from my parent's fiftieth anniversary celebration, he found something to do and left me in a darkened motel room for the day, to recover from too much time among my relatives, newly without defenses.

"Do you think I'm crazy?" I asked him one evening, when I had tried to share as much as I could and more than he could receive. "Strange and wondrous," he said, drawing me close. "But, no, not crazy." "I know this is asking an awful lot," I said. "Don't worry," he answered. "I won't wear out." In a new way, I experienced the tender faithfulness of God.

I talked to a nun who found my story odd, but saw no sign I had turned away from God. "It's going to be up to us," I thought. We had handled three teenagers, forced moves and women's liberation, but never before with such communication and grace. My deepest wish in the marriage had been to be understood. Here was my husband, with no preparation, understanding the inexpressible. It was like I had a chronic illness, but one that led into an enchanted land of shared adventure. "This relationship is of God," I said, and brought the call, the gifts and the desire into domestic life and marriage bed.

The desire was easy: Love is of God. I simply brought the sweet call to surrender into our shared claim on each other. Passion, worn by time and cares, bloomed in the context of a wider Love. My gift to God was also gift to Walter. His willingness to stay the course was gifted in our renewed love.

Domestic life was, in the end, simple, too. I needed simple. I took to heart John Wesley's question: "Do you love more because your heart and mind is fixed on Jesus Christ?" If not, why not? And always, what does love require? Embracing love, I found my way back into the dozens of daily doings that create life, nurture and home. Cleaning and procuring and preparing; cooking, listening and helping. Work that is never finished, rarely noticed, undervalued and unpaid. It was made to order for progress on a contemplative path.

There was still the matter of how to hold my disability, for it was as if I had lost my skin and was opened up, both to the outside world in all its turmoil and to an inner world of unpredictable, raw emotion. Activities I had taken for granted, like driving freeways, caring for small children, making phone calls and shopping trips, would catch me unawares and become impossible trials.

I held it all as doing what love requires by enfleshing Spirit. God was calling me to open to Spirit and my flesh, mind and body, was taxed and fragile, but willing to receive, in everything, more of God. Paul says we are being changed daily into the image and likeness of Christ. I held on to that and to the Incarnation, in which body stretched and bore all there is of Spirit.

All this was a long time ago. I am tougher now and my flesh can bear more. I hear its anguish, muted and far away, as I plunge ahead with whatever love requires. I never grew new skin. I became accustomed to living this way. I am somewhere on a contemplative path, without much notion of progress. God alone knows what's really going on. I travel this way as a married woman, enfleshing Spirit in the everyday and at evening coming home to Love.

CHAPTER SIX

Daybreak

by Robert A. Jonas

In November 1992, I made my third retreat at the L'Arche community of Daybreak. In a way, I limped to Toronto as one who was handicapped by grief. It had been only three months since Margaret and I had lost our daughter Rebecca to a premature birth and death. She had lived only four hours and died in our arms. Now, I would go to Daybreak, to be among my own kind, the broken and the marginalized.

I had often talked about the world of the severely handicapped with Henri Nouwen, who had given up his Yale and Harvard teaching appointments to be pastor in this L'Arche community. For those of us who pass for "normal," the handicapped can represent a threat. Our consumer culture and its symbiotic educational system create an abstract model person who is bright, slim and savvy. Anyone who is "somebody" has power, wealth, pleasure, beauty and eternal youth, attains infinite speed, completes fantastic numbers of projects and receives everlasting praise from inexhaustible sources. Trying to emulate these models often drives us so insistently that we become addicted to the fast life. We generally don't have time for those who are moving much more slowly on the muddy roads, in the shadows of modern life.

At L'Arche, popular models are turned on their heads. Here, people emphasize the gifts that come through suffering and through living with the wounded. Time, woven into the minutiae of dressing, eating, moving, brushing teeth and "signing," slows down. From the fast lane, things here look merely disfigured, crippled and useless. From the slow lane, one is encouraged to take another look, to seek out the details, delicacy and even beauty of what we thought was ugly.

One day, Henri took me along to have dinner at a L'Arche house in downtown Toronto. The one-story wooden house, with a small front yard and surrounding chain link fence, was nestled within a residential neighborhood. Here, six handicapped residents (called "core members") live with their helpers (called "assistants"). About twenty-five people gathered in the basement for an informal meal and to watch a slide presentation about another L'Arche house in Australia. Two visitors, one smiling, talkative core member with Down's Syndrome named Mary, and her assistant, Janet, greeted everyone. The celebratory spirit of the gathering did not surprise me. Over the years, I had learned that, at all L'Arche communities, birthdays, welcomes for visitors and new members, goodbye parties and liturgical holidays dot the weekly landscape. Tonight, everyone seemed eager to hear about the Australian community.

Before the presentation, Henri was to lead the group in a Catholic Mass. He asked me if I knew a shakuhachi piece that would be a good lead-in to the worship. As I brought the flute out of its leather case, two or three people asked what kind of instrument this was. Suddenly the shakuhachi was the center of attention. I told everyone about how this flute was handmade by my teacher, David Duncavage, who dug up the bamboo near Kyoto, Japan. I also spoke about the Buddhist and Christian practice of contemplative listening. One did not listen "outwardly" for a melody, but rather "inwardly," as if from the heart.

"I'm learning to play what is called honkyoku, or 'origin music,'" I said. "As far as we know, this flute music was brought to Japan from China in the eighth century. Sometimes, in Buddhist monasteries, it was practiced as a spiritual discipline, a kind of prayer. It is a music in which order cannot be imposed by the conscious mind, but must be discovered as one listens and watches in silence to the sudden swoops, dips and jumps of birds and land, dragonflies and crickets, streams, mud tracks and gusts of wind. In listening, we pay attention to the silence between the notes, as much as to the notes themselves." Everyone listened with great interest.

Then I brought the bamboo to my lips and played Kyo-rei, "Empty Bell." Two severely handicapped men slouched in their chairs, swinging their heads and eyes from side to side, unable to focus, and several others seemed uneasy in their afflicted bodies, squirming, pounding, rubbing and scraping their bodies against chairs and neighbors. Some, like Mary, sat very still, listening intently. When I blew Kyo-rei, I was struck by the immediate, comfortable silence in the room.

How strange this music must have sounded! But I sensed that Kyo-rei was being received. As I drew in each breath and blew each successive note, I saw within me countless scenes from institutions and homes for the handicapped where I had visited and worked, including L'Arche residences—scenes of silent waiting for, sitting alongside of, and simply being with, the profoundly handicapped. I wondered if the severely wounded understand more deeply than others the speechless atmosphere of the shakuhachi. Sometimes, as they lie in bed, waiting for someone to approach, they have nothing to do but listen in the lonely silence for their next breath.

On this night, many residents, both handicapped and their assistants, came up to me afterward to share how much they had appreciated the offering of music. I felt touched to be welcomed in such a warm manner. I remembered the warmth from my first visit to L'Arche in France several years before. The L'Arche spirit opens one's heart. Under its influence the distinction between handicapped and non-handicapped people melts away. On this night I felt as if I had a foot in both worlds. Here were plain people living together. Quite ordinary. But it was a very lovely sort of ordinary.

A week later we were back at the Daybreak retreat center called Dayspring. Twenty people had gathered for the Eucharist. A few big, vinyl-covered beanbag chairs were plopped among the wooden chairs for the most seriously disabled core members. One such person, a woman in her twenties, lay down across a bright red beanbag next to me. Rosey had Down's Syndrome and other serious problems that left her with little control over her arms and legs. She rolled her body back and forth over the soft vinyl and occasionally let out a powerful cry that sounded almost like a braying cow. She seemed to be more attentive during quiet parts of the service, especially during the prayers and the Eucharist. I couldn't tell if this behavior was intentional. Periodically Rosey turned to look at me with a blank stare. I wondered if she might be curious about me. But when I smiled at her, her face remained blank.

After the communion bread and wine had been passed around, everyone sat down, and I played a honkyoku piece. As I blew through the bamboo, I suddenly noticed that Rosey was making her "moo" sound at random intervals. At first I was annoyed, thinking that she was distracting people from the contemplative character of the music. A string of thoughts passed through my mind. "I hope someone will tell her to be quiet," I thought, and "The beauty of the music will be wasted unless someone takes her from the room."

I had wanted to offer everyone a special gift of music and silence, but it was not working. During the length of one prolonged note I decided that I would never have the patience of L'Arche's assistants and leaders. I could never survive the constant neediness of the handicapped. But then, to my astonishment, about halfway through the honkyoku, Rosey's "moo" seemed to fit in with the shakuhachi notes.

There was no way of telling whether Rosey intended to time her "moo" in relation to the honkyoku. And yet I began to feel her presence in "my" music. Suddenly, I and the shakuhachi were no longer the center of things. The center had moved into the middle of the group. It was as if both Rosey and the shakuhachi were sculpting the silence with their cries. The pitch of Rosey's "moo" resonated with a certain mournful note that occurs periodically throughout the honkyoku. Suddenly I felt that we were crying together for mercy. With a slight bend of my neck, a slight shading of the third hole on the flute, Rosey's note and mine found a pleasing and heartfelt resonance. Tears formed in my eyes. "Oh, how I wish my daughter Rebecca had lived," I thought. In my body, I felt a bond between Rosey and me, two wounded people suddenly transparent to Jesus' suffering on the cross. "Why have you forsaken me?" We were both living Jesus in us.

After the Mass, I watched Rosey's assistants talk to her and move her body into a more comfortable position. It seemed that Rosey could communicate with them in subtle ways. So I went over to Rosey to introduce myself. I touched her arm and said, "Hi, Rosey." Our eyes met for a split second. She looked down at my hand as if she were totally uninterested and then let her eyes drift dispassionately about the room. I didn't know if she felt any kind of connection to me. I waited a minute, watching her face, but her eyes never returned to mine. Had I been mistaken about our musical duet? Had I merely wished for, and projected, a connection that was never there? I realized that I might never know. But could the connection, and the empathy, have been "true" nonetheless? Somehow, I was convinced that beneath the conscious intellect, we had wandered into the same dark soul territory and had met for a common lament and a song.

As I prepared to leave Daybreak, I pondered the meaning of Rebecca's brief appearance. As she lay, naked and helpless in the neonatal intensive care unit, she, too, presented an expressionless, inscrutable face, bearing a look that was more than her mortal self. I saw in her face a striking, unsettling resemblance to the other faces in our family—Margaret's, Sam's and mine. It was as if, in looking into her dying face, I looked into a mirror, seeing both the "we" of our people and the beyondness, the edge of Nothing out of which we appear. Rebecca had come from Marg's body out of nowhere and disappeared into nature again, into the clouds, the ashes, the earth and the music. The sui-zen tradition of the shakuhachi was an earth music, testifying to a phenomenal, awesome flow of appearance and disappearance into nature and the Nothing that underlies it. In the Christian tradition, a perfect expression of the simultaneity of the apophatic and kataphatic.

In Zen and other Japanese arts, the personal and interpersonal dimensions of reality are meant to disappear into emptiness, so I sometimes feel as if I betray the sui-zen tradition when my honkyoku express grief for Rebecca. Isn't the point of the shakuhachi to convey equanimity and mystery, rather than mourning, protest and passion? Nevertheless, the Dayspring Eucharist had given me permission to experience the precious, paradoxical truth that Saint John of the Cross has so beautifully conveyed in his poetry—in silence is God's music, in death is God's life, and in our mourning is God's grief.

On my last evening at Daybreak, a strong cool wind had come up out of the Arctic north. We could barely hear its whispered movements at the basement windows. Into the silence after communion, I played a Shirabe (panting breath) piece of honkyoku. Shirabe notes are blown in rhythmic, breathy gusts, echoing the weather in some northern mountains where there are Japanese sui-zen monasteries. For one moment during the piece, my thinking slipped over the horizon and "I" disappeared into the silence between the notes.

I only noticed this transformation later, as I was about to leave Daybreak. What had happened in that Shirabe at the evening Eucharist? It seemed that in the moment of "no-mind" there was only a long, winding, forested valley, untouched by human purposes, with only the wind rushing down the slopes of the surrounding mountains and over the tree tops and marsh grasses. But then, in the midst of that valley, a person appeared in my heart's eye, singing something I could not understand. Something haunting and exquisite. Who appeared? There was no distinct image, but I sensed that it was someone wise and humble, someone who stands in the original doorway where everything appears out of Nothing. Perhaps it was Christ, or Buddha, singing with the wind in the valley.

That night it began to rain. Before going to bed, I walked into the darkened chapel to play one final honkyoku in thankfulness to the Daybreak community and the sui-zen tradition. Letting my face and lips relax, the notes came from somewhere deep within. For an instant, the lowest note that the shakuhachi can play became a sacred plow, turning all my thoughts into the muddy earth.

PART TWO

GUIDELINES FOR GROWING AS A LAY CONTEMPLATIVE

CHAPTER SEVEN

A Roman Catholic Theology of Lay Contemplation

by Mary Frohlich

Many dimensions contribute to a person's affirmation that he or she has a contemplative calling. Components may include contemplative experiences, contemplative practices, a contemplative identity, a contemplative life-style—each of which may be manifested in widely varying ways. With the raw material of gifts, opportunities and choices, each individual mixes these components in a unique way to create a personal contemplative way. Thus, there is no one face of the contemplative; contemplatives may look, act, talk, think and pray very differently from one another.

■ A THEOLOGICAL ANTHROPOLOGY FOR LAY CONTEMPLATION

An underlying theological principle is essential if we are to begin making any sense of this confusing diversity. That principle is the affirmation that human beings are created with a contemplative core. We are created to love God, to know God, to be in union with God. Our truest and most original being lives in deepest intimacy with God, wholly transparent to God and wholly motivated by divine love. Theologically, there is a sense in which *every* human being is created to be a contemplative—that is, one who lives in complete openness to God in every dimension of his or her being. On the basis of this theological principle, we will explore the various dimensions of the contemplative vocation: experience, practice, identity and life-style.

We can define contemplative experience as awareness—whether fleeting or habitual—of that most foundational, most original depth

45

of being. Contemplative teacher William Shannon, for example, describes contemplative experience as conscious awareness of the being-in-God's-presence that we are.[1] We always are, always have been and always will be in God's presence, and if we were not we would not be at all. Because this is our most foundational reality, contemplative experience is potentially available to every human being, at all times and in every circumstance. It can, and does, "happen" to people without any preparation and while they are engaged in pursuits that are not concerned with seeking it. It is always a grace—that is, it is God who gives Godself, not we who grasp God.

We are not always aware of this most fundamental reality of our existence. The obstacles to this awareness include some for which we are culpable ("sins") and some which simply are there, without our knowing why. While contemplation is essentially a grace, a discipline of contemplative practice is also a significant factor in preparing the way and making it possible for it to become an established dimension of an individual's spiritual life. Contemplative prayer practices are based on the principle that waking up to contemplative awareness is not a matter of focusing on God as an object, but rather of emptying out and opening up to the gift of being at one with God that is always being given at the ground of our being. Since it is a gift, we cannot make it happen; yet it does seem as if long-term fidelity to spiritual practices that assist in the emptying out of object-focused consciousness and the opening up of deeper, more silent dimensions of one's being prepares the way for such moments.

This interplay of grace and discipline means that it is difficult to make hard and fast statements about how, when and where people will experience contemplative prayer. Some may experience many moments of conscious contemplative awareness with seemingly little discipline, while others may practice much discipline and yet apparently have little of the grace of such breakthroughs. Probably the most common pattern, however, is for an individual to practice a moderate discipline of an object-focused type of prayer (for example, reflective, imaginative or devotional modes) for some time, with occasional refreshing glimpses of contemplative awareness. Then a time comes when something changes. The ways of prayer that have been so satisfying begin to seem dry and empty. A period of painful struggle ensues, eventually followed by a more consistent experience of a contemplative, non-object-focused form of prayer.

Within the contemplative traditions efforts have been made to identify the characteristics of such a time when a shift is occurring from an experience of prayer that is object-focused to a more contemplative way. John of the Cross spells out three signs to look for:

> The first is the realization that one cannot make discursive meditation or receive satisfaction from it as before. Dryness is now the outcome of fixing the senses on subjects that formerly provided satisfaction....
>
> The second sign is an awareness of a disinclination to fix the imagination or sense faculties [intentionally] on other particular objects, exterior or interior....
>
> The third and surest sign is that a person likes to remain alone in loving awareness of God, without particular considerations, in interior peace and quiet and repose, and without acts and exercises (at least discursive, those in which one progresses from point to point) of the intellect, memory and will. Such a one prefers to remain only in the general, loving awareness and knowledge we mentioned, without any particular knowledge or understanding.[2]

In the understanding of John of the Cross, these signs are likely to be observed during the period that he terms the "active night of the spirit." This time is characterized by a wrenching process of letting go of attachment to all that has previously occupied one's mental and emotional attention. The active discipline of such letting go, however, is fruitless if the person has not really arrived at the point of passage to contemplation, for unless one's emptying-out is filled by the grace of contemplative awareness of being-in-God, it remains barren.

Once again we are reminded to remain humble in our efforts to systematize the interplay between grace and discipline. Nevertheless, John's careful discussion makes the point that not every Christian—and not even every Christian who is serious about cultivating the spiritual life—undergoes this passage into a more consistent experience of contemplative prayer. Every human being is potentially open to the contemplative dimension; many people have had sporadic conscious experiences of it; among these, some (but not all) experience the transition to a form of prayer that is more or less consistently contemplative.

At this point we have to thicken the plot a bit by acknowledging a difficulty with the way I have so far presented contemplation. The problem is that words such as "experience" and "awareness" are not entirely adequate to the reality of contemplation. The reality of being in God's presence is so fundamental to our existence that it is far more—and less—than an experience. Ultimately the core of contemplation is faith, which may be accompanied by total or near-total affective and intellectual darkness. In this sense, the person who lives totally in faith may be more rooted in contemplation than the one who has a great many profound feelings and insights related to being in God's presence. Thérèse of Lisieux is an example of a contemplative who spent the last eighteen months of her life in this kind of spiritual darkness. The transition of which John of the Cross speaks is in some ways more a passage to "unknowing" than to "knowing."

What, then, does it mean to "be a contemplative"? Because of the ambiguity of contemplative experience, there is little value—and much danger—in attempting to pin down who is "more contemplative" at the level of experience. It is more accurate simply to say that some individuals discover and claim a contemplative identity that becomes central in their self-understanding and their way of being in the world. Psychologist Erik Erikson has spoken of identity as having two core dimensions: first, an inner sense of one's own firmness, centeredness and historical continuity; second, an outwardly focused sense of having a place, a role, a set of skills and competencies, within a specific sociocultural environment.[3] A person who claims an identity as a contemplative is affirming that in both the interior and the social realms, his or her sense of selfhood is centered around experiences and/or practices of contemplation.

Contemplative life-style is still another distinct dimension. It might be defined as one in which choices about daily schedule, participation in ecclesial communities, engagement in ministry, way of earning a living and other significant life issues are shaped by the priority of the contemplative dimension. Concretely, the ways in which a lay contemplative life-style is being expressed vary widely. Some establish hermitages in remote areas; others live with spouses and children in cities or suburbs. Some hold demanding jobs; others find a way to earn a sparse living quietly. Some seek others of like mind with whom to associate; others guard their solitude more carefully than gold. Some individuals practice their contemplative life-style quietly and unobtrusively, while others are called to make it a public witness. While there are no absolutes as to how such a life-style has to be played out—that is, not all involve celibacy, not all take place in cloisters or other quiet locations—the contemplative life-style does involve giving an identifiable priority to availability for contemplative experience and practice.

Even though it is not appropriate for lay contemplatives to imitate the life-style of religious, there is still much to be learned from the wisdom of past contemplatives. For example, the thirteenth-century "Rule of Saint Albert," which forms the foundation of the Carmelite way of life, includes a phrase that is a classic distillation of basic principles for a contemplative life-style: "The brothers will remain in or near their cells, meditating on the word of God day and night, unless called forth by some other just occupation."[4] Recent commentators on the Rule note that the "cells" where this solitary practice takes place are the units of a common life in which an oratory for daily Eucharist forms the physical center, and there are also other shared buildings and functions. Thus, the context of this summary statement is a description of a community life of mutual service centered around the Eucharist.[5]

While the specifics will differ, many lay contemplatives can resonate with this injunction of a preference for solitude, a commitment to daily contemplative practice and the flexibility of a charitable heart that responds to the real needs of others—all taking place within some form of community life. In the case of the lay contemplative the latter may be the parish or a religious community house, but it is also likely to find an equally important center in family, neighborhood, friendship circle or support group.

Traditionally, the Christian contemplative life-style has been deeply woven with the liturgical and sacramental rituals of the Church. More often than not this takes a significantly different form for the lay contemplative. As lay theologian Elizabeth Dreyer put it in a recent interview, for the laity (and increasingly for all people today) God and God's action are first found in the world and in the mundane activities of daily life. Ecclesial liturgy and sacraments are experienced as celebrating and enhancing this permeating divine presence, rather than as being its primary point of entry into human life.[6] At the same time, many lay contemplatives develop a deep sensitivity to symbol and ritual, and often they are at the forefront of efforts to create new ways to weave them into the everyday lives of family and community.

As indicated earlier, these four dimensions of contemplative being (experience, practice, identity, life-style) present themselves in a unique mix in each contemplative's life. For example, some may have a great deal of contemplative experience without an urgency to structure contemplative practice or to claim a contemplative identity or life-style; others may practice in a disciplined way and strongly claim contemplative identity and life-style, yet rarely be gifted with contemplative experience. Since the core of *all* aspects of contemplative being is the grace of God who created us to share divine life and who gives the fullness of that gift to each in unique ways, no particular combination of the dimensions should be regarded as a cause for either shame or glory; each is simply gift.

■ AN ECCLESIOLOGY FOR LAY CONTEMPLATION

At this point, it will be helpful to introduce a second theological principle that is essential to understanding the contemplative vocation. The persons we are created and called to be exist not only in relationship of love with God, but also and equally in a relationship of love with our fellow human beings. Whatever gifts we receive through both nature and grace are intended to be used to build up the communion of all human beings in and with God. Hence, "being a contemplative" is a charism—a gift of grace for the Church.

It is sometimes mistakenly presumed that the contemplative way is inherently an individualistic one, focused primarily on one's own development in relationship to God. Indeed, every profession or lifestyle has "occupational hazards," and it may be true that a leaning toward individualism can easily creep into a contemplative's life. For Christians, however, a gauge of the authenticity of one's contemplative experience is the degree to which it leads one more deeply into commitment to building up the community in love. If this is not the direction in which one is moving, it may be evidence that one is not growing in union with the God who, in Christ, has been totally poured out in love on behalf of the whole people of God. Teresa of Avila, for example, wrote:

> I see, Sisters, that if we fail in love of neighbor we are lost.... When you see yourselves lacking in this love, even though you have devotion and gratifying experiences that make you think you have reached this stage [of union], and you experience some little suspension in the prayer of quiet,...believe me you have not reached union.[7]

The question of the character and role of the laity in general, and of the lay contemplative in particular, must be considered within this basic framework. Whatever the phenomenon of lay contemplation may mean when viewed in sociological or cultural terms, within a Christian theological framework its meaning only comes into focus in relation to how God is building up the Church through the charisms and offices that are being given to particular Christians. A charism, by definition, is not given to everyone. Just as some members of the body of Christ build up the communion by being preachers, others by being teachers, others by being administrators, and still others by joining contemplative religious communities, so some may do so by being lay contemplatives.

Many theological and ideological currents swirl around the question of the laity. One aspect of this is the difference between Roman Catholic and Protestant understandings of this terminology. For some Protestants the term *lay* is little used within Church conversations, since structurally defined distinctions between Christians in official ministerial roles and others are minimal. For other Protestants there is a distinction between ordained and non-ordained, but both groups share the life-style of marriage and participation in all aspects of the secular world.

Within Roman Catholicism, on the other hand, celibacy and priesthood are closely bound together, and there is the additional category of celibate "religious" who also have a life-style different from that of the majority of Christians. In common parlance among Catholics, "laity" has most often referred to those not belonging to these celibate groups. Yet with the Second Vatican Council (1962-65) a major revision of this mentality began shaking up old assumptions.

After the Council a basic debate ensued over whether the term *laity* properly refers to nothing different from the biblically preferable "people of God" (that is, all the faithful), or whether it refers to a category of Christians that should be carefully distinguished from the categories of "clerics" and "religious." An examination of the biblical and early Christian evidence, in fact, finds that sometimes the Greek *laos* or "people" did indeed refer inclusively to all the people without distinction, but that in other places it was used to refer to the people as distinct from their consecrated leaders.[8] A stronger biblical argument for a radically egalitarian ecclesiological vision derives from the fact that the most theologically rich terms used for the followers of Jesus, including "disciples," "elect," "saints" and "believers," do not make any distinctions of categories—all Christians are included. The terminology of distinctions, on the other hand, such as "servant" (*diakonos* or deacon), "elder" (*presbyteros* or presbyter) and "supervisor" (*episkopos* or bishop), takes up cultural terminology that was not originally theologically based.[9]

One approach to dealing with this somewhat ambiguous evidence, then, is to level the distinctions; another is to sharpen them. In relation to the question of contemplative life, the egalitarian tendency may tend to reject any reflection on distinct needs or gifts of "lay contemplatives"—thus short-circuiting efforts to articulate a theological basis for new ways of living a contemplative vocation. The distinguishing tendency, on the other hand, may so emphasize defining the different characters of contemplative life inside and outside of the canonically established cloister as to cast doubt on the validity of one or the other. Often the latter reflection is tainted by a defensive instinct, either on the part of those dedicated to canonical cloistered contemplative life *or* on the part of those who have rejected this way for themselves.

A 1988 article by Giovanni Magnani, in which he propounds an essentially egalitarian view as the foundation for making clarifying distinctions, offers a perspective that I find helpful for our purposes. After carefully analyzing the key references to "lay" and "laity" in the documents of Vatican II, Magnani concludes that fundamentally the Council rejected making "laity" into a category of Christians contrasted to clergy and/or religious. Rather, the documents reveal an effort to identify the "layperson" as equivalent to the *christifideles* or "member of Christ's faithful"—in short, the Christian. In this perspective all Christians are first and foremost laypersons—that is, members of the "people of God" (*laos*). Differentiations, including those which create clergy and religious, are secondary and are on a different logical level from the inclusive category of "laity."[10]

Despite his clear rejection of the approach of assigning different tasks to different categories of Christians, Magnani does not abandon the quest to articulate a "specific character" of the laity. The Council's larger agenda, he believes, was to clarify that the primary work of the whole Church is "the task of ordering temporal things toward God, of taking them up to transform them in Christ, and of the recapitulation that involves the whole of the created order."[11] This affirmation that the Church's chief role is to serve the transformation of the temporal and created order is a fairly radical paradigm shift from previous models, and it has a profound effect on how the role of the laity is viewed. Simply put, full and intense engagement in that task *is* the "specific character" of the member of Christ's faithful, that is, the layperson.

The layperson, then, is one in and through whom this primary work of the Church—the work of lifting up and transforming the whole created world—can reach its fullness. The laity are placed at the center of the Church, as those within whom God's transformation of the created world is most intensely being realized. Creation itself, as well as the secular activities involved in governing and developing its potential, is viewed positively as the realm within which God is at work. Magnani notes that this is quite different from earlier eras, in which:

> The theology of creation and of Christ as being all in all were largely stifled by a theology and a spirituality that were guided by clerics and monks who in turn were biased in favor of a theology of redemption that therefore appears rather unbalanced, concentrating as it does more on the "not yet" of the kingdom and a certain flight from the world rather than on a proper appreciation of the lay state.[12]

It is important to emphasize that the newness in this theology is not meant to be simply a reversed elitism, so that whereas in earlier theologies it appeared "better" to be a cleric or a religious, now it is "better" not to be. Rather, the clerical and religious states are now seen as subsequent specifications of the more fundamental "layness" of the Christian faithful. Clerics and religious, like all Christians, participate in the transformation of the world in ways appropriate to their particular offices and charisms; but their clerical or religious state does not, *per se*, afford them any greater or more important role.

These considerations do not entirely resolve the practical problem of how to use the terms *lay* and *laity*. In what follows I try to use these terms to refer inclusively to the Christian people as called to active presence within all aspects of the created world, prior to any ecclesiastical distinctions such as sacramental orders or canonical vows. While this definition does not exclude members of the clergy and religious institutes, the intended emphasis is on Christian life that is *not* inserted within those categories. If the reader finds a degree of unresolved tension remaining in this use of language (as I confess I do), it probably reflects the continuing tensions in our ecclesial experience and practice. The best we can do, perhaps, is to attempt to enhance the creative dimensions of these tensions, while minimizing their destructive potential.

Lay contemplatives are Christians who experience a call to give concerted attention to the contemplative dimension, within a theological and practical framework of openness to the world and active engagement in its transformation. While this way of living the contemplative life does not change the practical reality of the need for certain times and places of silence, solitude and separation in order to develop contemplatively, it places this need within a theological framework that is oriented toward participation in the secular world rather than withdrawal from it.

■ A CHRISTOLOGY FOR LAY CONTEMPLATION

Any Christian way of life is a discipleship of Jesus. To be a disciple is in some way to follow, to imitate, to be conformed to, one's teacher. Yet exactly who Jesus is and what being his disciple asks of us have been understood in a great many different ways within Christian tradition. We need to explore here how we can envision Christ as the paradigm for the lay contemplative life.

In a 1987 article on John Paul II's theology of the laity, Joe Holland contrasts two basic perspectives on how God operates in the world. In the classical view, God is envisioned as masculine and is transcendent over nature, which is envisioned as feminine. Within the Church, clergy share in the masculine, transcendent character of God while the laity (who, within this theology, are those who are neither ordained nor in religious vows) have a feminine, submissive character. In the secular world, however, the laity are called to participate in God's masculine transcendence over the natural and historical world. This classical view leads to a Christology in which both Christ's maleness and his hierarachical dominance are central. Christ is the "head" who makes all decisions and hands them down to subordinates through a chain of command that passes from pope to bishops to priests to laity. A good disciple is above all obedient within this chain of command. A lay disciple is called to accept a peripheral and submissive role within the Church, while taking an active role in the transformation of nature and history.

While this classical theology does not exclude the possibility of a lay contemplative vocation, it also does not encourage it. Contemplation is pure "feminine" receptivity to the transcendent God. Its proper place is in the religious life. The laity's proper vocation, on the other hand, is active, "masculine" transformation of the world. In some rare cases these vocations may be mixed, but this is seen more as an "exception that proves the rule" than as an emerging new paradigm.

Holland calls the contrasting perspective the "American post-modern view." He describes it this way:

> The American post-modern perspective proceeds from the bottom up in a framework of immanence, adds the dimension of God as symbolically feminine giving life from below, proceeds to the unfolding creativity of the universe's ecological dynamism, and lastly comes to humanity as the emerging consciousness within nature, all perceived in a framework of ecological, human, divine communion.[13]

In this perspective, God's immanence within nature and history is as central as God's transcendence. The fullness of God's life is manifested in a mutual embrace of immanence and transcendence, rather than the dominance of one over the other. The full equality-in-difference of male and female is a crucial symbol of this mutual embrace.

The Christology that emerges within this perspective is very different from the classical Christology. Here, Christ's role as representative of the transcendent God is less significant than his identity as the human being within whom divinity and materiality embrace in radical fullness and mutuality. Rather than being the head of the Church who makes all its decisions, he is the loving heart within whom all—body and soul, sinner and saint—are welcomed and joined together in the great communion of the Church.

To belong to Christ, then, is not so much to take up one's place in a chain of command as it is to give oneself wholeheartedly over to cocreating this welcoming communion with him. The Christ to whom the Christian becomes a disciple is not so much concerned about setting up boundaries and structures as about healing all divisions so that the whole creation is reconciled in love. Each office and charism in the Church accomplishes this in a different way, but none has an inherent primacy; rather, "Whoever wants to be first must be last of all and servant of all" (Mark 9:35).

In this Christology, the contemplative vocation is an intense, intimate participation in Christ's life and work. In this view, it makes sense that people from every walk of life will be called to the contemplative vocation—for only in this way can every nook and cranny of creation be directly touched and reconciled by a member of Christ's body.

■ ELEMENTS OF A SPIRITUALITY FOR LAY CONTEMPLATION

As there was in Jesus' life, there is both an emptiness and a fullness in the contemplative way. The emptiness can be imaged in Jesus' words, "I am the gate" (John 10:9). To be a gate or a doorway for others is to become empty so that no obstacle stands in the way of others' entry into fullness. Contemplative emptiness is a sharing in Jesus' self-emptying, which came to a climax on the cross. There is a deeply interior dimension of this emptiness, but more often than not it also has ramifications for the contemplative's physical, psychological and social life as well. For many lay contemplatives, it may take the shape of misunderstanding and scorn from one's closest compatriots, neverending urgings (interior and exterior) to dissipate one's energy through all sorts of "important" activities, or simply the drain of the inner turmoil that inevitably accompanies certain passages of the spiritual life—all borne without the security of an assured title or the support of a canonically bolstered discipline of life.

Contemplative fullness, on the other hand, is allowing one's whole being—physical, psychological, social as well as spiritual—to be re-created into a capacious dwelling place that, like Christ, embraces all within a loving communion. Sacramental practice and imagination, which are especially well-developed within the Roman Catholic communion, offer rich resources for this graced project of allowing the whole creation to be a place of God's presence. Some form of participation in ritual, symbol and sacrament are essential to the development of this contemplative fullness. Yet the lay contemplative, whose life-style normally includes full engagement in the secular world, is also called to develop this dimension of the contemplative vocation in new ways.

A window into some implications of the emerging perspective is to observe the shift in perspectives on the human body. Many classical Christian spiritualities tended to take an athletic approach to controlling the body, operating out of the belief that without severe discipline the natural tendencies of the body are opposed to contemplative development. In a more wholistic spirituality the natural tendencies of the body are believed to be *toward* radical fullness of life and contemplation; that development is opposed by artificial and pathological repressions that paralyze or distort the positive potential of the body. Christ, who lived, died and rose as an embodied human being, is model and guide for a complete reconciliation of the body to fullness of life. Hence, spiritual discipline is understood not so much as ascetic control of the body as a liberating therapy.

The actual bodily practices may be similar: fasting, silence, solitude, meditation and many other traditional contemplative disciplines can be practiced within either framework of meaning. The new mentality, however, also opens the door for many other forms of bodywork to become a significant dimension of the contemplative journey. Yoga, breathwork, martial arts, massage, jogging and many other approaches to lessening bodily rigidity and opening up more subtle dimensions of bodily experience are frequently advocated by serious spiritual seekers today.

A major change in attitude toward sexuality accompanies this shift in attitudes toward the body. It is no longer assumed that celibacy is the only or best way to pursue the contemplative life. Rather, the deep relational potential of the marital relationship, including its physical sexual expression, is seen as a contemplative way in itself. While a significant number of contemplatives will still experience a call to celibacy as the best context for developing their contemplative experience, this may no longer be the most common scenario of contemplative development.

On a broader scale, contemplative life today is much more likely than it was in generations past to be envisioned as integrally linked with action on behalf of social justice or ecology. This, too, is connected to the change in attitudes to the body: The bodies of the poor, the oppressed, the tortured and finally the body of the earth itself are affirmed as having sacred value, both in themselves and in relation to the contemplative vocation. A positive valuing of one's own body, which has its origin, its particular characteristics and its ongoing nurturance from its connections with the earth and with other people's bodies, opens out to a spirituality of solidarity, compassion and care. While the concrete actions flowing from this will take different forms in the lives of different individuals, it is noteworthy that today there is often a significant overlap between those committed to a contemplative life and those committed to action on behalf of social and ecological justice.

Rather than defining lay contemplation as a rejection of earlier ways of living the contemplative life, we can define it as a development of a theology of the transformation of creation and the temporal world through the action of Christ in his people. Whereas previous spiritualities were usually deeply imbued with an assumption that the best way to dedicate oneself entirely to God was through withdrawal (to the degree possible) from secular and material engagements, contemporary theologies affirm "the world" as the locus of God's presence and action. Contemplative development, then, has everything to do with a deepening of one's responsible presence in and for the world. The lay contemplative movement is an integral expression of this emerging new paradigm.

■ NOTES

[1] William H. Shannon, *Silence on Fire* (New York: Crossroad, 1995), chapter 2.

[2] John of the Cross, *Ascent of Mount Carmel* (Washington, D.C.: Institute of Carmelite Studies, 1991), II:13, 2-4.

[3] Erik H. Erikson, *Identity: Youth and Crisis* (New York: W.W. Norton, 1968).

[4] Bede Edwards, ed., *The Rule of St. Albert* (London: Carmelite Book Service, 1973).

[5] In M. Malhall, ed., *Albert's Way* (Rome: Institutum Carmelitanam, 1989), pp. 94-132.

[6] Elizabeth Dreyer, *National Catholic Reporter*, 1996.

[7] Teresa of Avila, *The Interior Castle* (New York: Doubleday Image, 1972), V:3,12.

[8] I. de la Potterie, "L'origine et le sens primitif du mot 'laic,'" *Nouvelle revue theologique 80* (1958), 840-53.

[9] Giovanni Magnani, S.J., "Does the So-Called Theology of the Laity Possess a Theological Status?," in Rene Latourelle, ed., *Vatican II: Assessment and Perspectives, 25 Years Later (1962-1987)* (New York: Paulist, 1998), pp. 568-633.

[10] Magnani, p. 588.

[11] Magnani, pp. 600-601.

[12] Magnani, p. 578.

[13] Joe Holland, "John Paul II on the Laity in Society: The Spiritual Transformation of Modern Culture," *Social Thought* 13/2-3 (1987), pp. 87-103.

CHAPTER EIGHT

The Formation of the Everyday Contemplative

by Stephen K. Hatch

In our time, increasing numbers of everyday people are being drawn to contemplative practice. Stress in the workplace and home, the breakneck pace and complexity of the "information age" and a growing lack of connection to the natural world drive many to seek a life of greater silence, peace and simplicity. People hunger for the sacred within the ordinary details of life; they search for a way to make mundane existence transparent to its divine core.

Current interest in the Christian contemplative tradition was sparked by the writings of Trappist monk Thomas Merton in the fifties and sixties. It has been fanned into flame by Trappists Thomas Keating and Basil Pennington, Benedictines David Steindl-Rast and John Main, Irish Jesuit William Johnston, Dominican-turned-Episcopalian Matthew Fox and a growing number of spiritual guides. The *Classics of Western Spirituality* series from Paulist Press has made many mystical classics available in fine translation. In addition, many Eastern gurus, roshis, lamas and their Western students are contributing the perspectives of Asian contemplatives. Most recently, a new generation of Native Americans is adding its voice as well. Writers Marsha Sinetar in *Ordinary People as Monks and Mystics* and Duane Elgin in *Voluntary Simplicity* have chronicled modern attempts by ordinary people to live a more contemplative life.

Everyone has the potential to become a fully transformed mystic. Since I do not believe in separating everyday contemplatives from a class of "professional contemplatives" (that is, "religious"), I deliberately refrain from using the terms *lay* or *laity* when discussing everyday contemplatives. Within the Christian tradition, the Radical Reformation holds the most egalitarian perspective with regard to contemplative social structure within the spiritual community. Quakers, Mennonites, the Brethren and some evangelical charismatics view the entire community as a "kingdom of priests" where there is no ecclesial hierarchy.

Douglas Steere articulates Quaker experience:

> In an age of the rediscovery of the infinite worth of the "commonest he" [the seventeenth century] George Fox and his followers invited men and women of all conditions into the freedom of a new corporate fellowship. There, without the authority of an infallible church or an infallible Bible or the ever-present authority of a paid clergy, those in this fellowship might gather together in meetings on the basis of silence and obedience in order to assist each other in coming into the presence of Christ within, and where they might come to know each other in that which is eternal. The group sat together waiting on God to gather them inwardly, and *all* shared in the responsibility for helping the meeting to become a vessel of the Holy Spirit. It has often been said that the Quakers, who were fiercely "lay" in character, had in a sense "abolished the laity" in that with *all* members potential ministers, they were the most radical implementers of "the priesthood of all believers."[1]

Friends did not traditionally use the term *contemplative*, but their valuing of silence and the interior life places them firmly within the Christian mystical tradition. In this egalitarian spirituality, leaders *do* emerge from within the community, but any authority they hold comes only by virtue of a transformed life, not because of any ecclesial title or academic training.

An egalitarian view is important today, especially given the fact that in many classical Christian spiritualities the fullness of contemplation often appears to be reserved for an elite few. John of the Cross, for example, made this comment about why some spiritual seekers do not seem to enter into contemplation:

> God places them in this night [of the senses] solely to exercise and humble them. But He does not do so in order to lead them to the life of the spirit, which is contemplation. For God does not bring to contemplation all those who purposely exercise themselves in the way of the spirit, not even half. Why? He best knows.[2]

The danger of such an apparent exclusivism is that it may prevent some people from coming into an awareness of their full potential as contemplatives. Instead they focus on *someone else*—Father X or Sister Y—whom they view as having a superior potential for spiritual growth. This may cheapen their unique graces as everyday contemplatives. We tend to shirk our own spiritual call by projecting it onto some leader. But each of us must realize that no one else can replicate our unique contribution to the evolution of spirituality.

Although the foregoing discussion may seem to fault Christianity on this point, it should also be pointed out that the mystical tradition in Christianity, more than in any other world religion, leaves judgment concerning a person's degree of spiritual attainment to the Divine rather than to some human master. In this sense, the Christian way is potentially as egalitarian as any of the world spiritualities.

I have spent the past fifteen years experimenting with a contemplative life-style in the midst of the everyday world. I have attempted to balance meditation practice, raising children, study, wilderness hiking, teaching spirituality and manual labor—with varying success. This is the context out of which I write. My goal in this chapter is to articulate contemplative practices adequate to the sensual, nonmonastic context in which the everyday contemplative lives.

Without the practice of contemplative disciplines, growth along the spiritual path stagnates unless one is specially gifted. In any human endeavour, excelling requires constant attention and practice as necessary conditions. The spiritual life is no exception. The early Christian desert tradition referred to discipline as the means whereby we simply *remain* in the divine artist's workshop so the divine image can be painted like an icon within us. The pursuit of distraction is like jumping off the easel before the artist can apply the next brush stroke. In another metaphor, discipline is compared to shutting the door of a sauna so the steam can concentrate. Distraction is like reducing the spiritual heat by continually opening the door.

For monastics, the monastery provides a rule of life that acts as a spiritual trellis to train them in their growth toward the Light. Without the advantage of such a rule, everyday contemplatives have to develop their own set of disciplines. It will be tailor-made to suit the schedule, living situation and temperament of each individual or family member. Here I list some of the practices that I have found indispensible in the contemplative quest.

Regular Practice of Contemplative Prayer. Practices such as zazen, centering prayer or *shamatha* (a practice of resting deeply in silence and tranquility) train the meditator to release all thoughts and perceptions in order to discover the spacious divine silence out of which they emerge at every moment. Perhaps contemplatives who live in close and frequent communion with the natural world—such as Native Americans in their traditional environment—connect so thoroughly with the spaciousness present in the landscape that they don't need a formal meditation practice to develop the awareness of interior spaciousness. But most of us don't fall naturally into silent vastness; we have to cultivate it. A standard dose of contemplative prayer consists of two periods of twenty minutes each day. Early mornings before work, lunchtimes and evenings are all potential times for those with nine-to-five schedules. If you feel you don't have the time, consider reducing time spent in activities such as excessive television watching or overcommitment to others' needs. Give extra time to meditation on weekends or during one-day personal retreats. If family members complain of time spent in meditation away from them and their needs, remind them with humor that you will be easier to live with if meditation is practiced regularly.

Scheduled Solitude. Solitude is one of the most important ingredients of the spiritual life because it puts one in touch with one's inner resources and interior silence. Moreover, time spent in the solitude of nature adds an indispensable ingredient not found in buildings. The divine presence communicating from within nature is often the only thing that can reveal the vastness of the spirit and the pettiness, by comparison, of much of our human worry. I'm always amazed at how easily I forget these truths when I'm away from nature. So many times I arrive in the hills for an afternoon of solitude and find myself exclaiming spontaneously: "Oh yes, *this* is what is really real!" Thomas Merton writes of the importance of nature's solitude: "When you are by yourself, you soon get tired of your craziness. It is too exhausting. It does not fit in with the eminent sanity of trees, birds, water, sky."[3]

The solitude of nature has the ability to awaken interior silence in a way that nothing else can. Henry David Thoreau says: "We walk to lakes to see our serenity reflected in them."[4] Wayne Simsic, the author of *Natural Prayer*, reveals his approach: "How then do you pray in the silence of nature? Go to the landscape that appeals to you, let the silence of the landscape resonate within your being, and let God's presence fill your heart and become prayer."[5] I live at the foot of the Colorado Rockies, so I'm able to schedule frequent time alone in the hills. In the summer I arrange one all-day hike or weekend camping trip per week in addition to several afternoons on my retreat spot amidst fragrant ponderosa pines at the top of a nearby foothill. In the winter, although it is easier to lose perspective when the wildlands are colder and more inaccessible, a snowstorm hitting town brings the silence of nature to our civilized world.

If a person lives in a big city with little or no access to wilderness, a city park or a roadside tree can bring divine peace closer. Even a walk around the block can open up interior spaciousness. The exercise alone tends to free the self from its entrapment within the constricted ego. Extended retreat time—perhaps an entire day or weekend—should be scheduled at least once a month. If family members complain, encourage them to schedule a day for themselves to do whatever they want and offer to take on added chores during that time if need be.

The Practice of Mindfulness. Mindfulness practice, or *vipashyana*, involves several levels. At first, one trains the mind simply to attend to whatever perception or thought is present in the moment. One notices that the sky is blue or that one is having angry thoughts or that one is feeling tightness in the stomach or an ease in one's walk. This conscious attention is itself quite an accomplishment, since normally we act out of anger without even being aware that we feel anger, or we go through the day without even knowing what phase the moon is in. Gunilla Norris, in her book of mindfulness meditations entitled *Being Home*, reveals a mindful attitude in her meditation on dusting. She sees dusting as an opportunity to caress and get to know all of the textures in her home. She even calls this a sort of "love-making."[6] This attitude reveals an exquisite degree of mindful attention to the mundane details of everyday life.

A second level of mindfulness involves moving beyond bare attention into a deeper awareness. One takes the vast silence one has encountered in *shamatha* or tranquility meditation or centering prayer and surrounds the perceptions with it. Instead of holding onto one's perceptions, one releases them, allowing them to arise out of the silence one has brought to consciousness. Rilke describes this process beautifully in a poem:

Space reaches *from* us and construes the world:
to know a tree, in its true element,
throw inner space around it, from that pure
abundance in you. Surround it with restraint.
It has no limits. Not till it is held
in your renouncing is it truly there.[7]

This practice allows the contemplative to remain in awe at the echo quality of perceptions, especially as he or she identifies ever more deeply with the vast silence. To facilitate this awareness at first, silently repeat the word *echo* every time a perception arises out of the silence. Consciously attend to perceptions whenever you can throughout the day. If you are in the natural world, speak the names of things—rock, tree, flower or sky—and release these sounds to be seen for what they really are: presences arising out of the vast spacious silence of the natural landscape.

A third level of mindfulness occurs when the contemplative learns to let go even of the conscious effort involved in the first two levels. Then one can say (as Buddhists do) that awareness occurs without a discrete person who is aware. Like the sunlight diffused throughout the blue sky, here there is a union of perceiver and perceived in the limitless expanse of consciousness itself. As Zen master Dennis Genpo Merzel says, "When you are no longer clinging, then you can see things clearly as they are, without the observer. Then there is just seeing, just hearing. There is no one here, just space!"[8] In Franciscan priest Richard Rohr's image, this is the contemplative's dissolving into the awareness that it is God who is lost in thinking the world into existence; an entering into the spacious bliss of the mind of God.[9] Another example of this level of mindfulness is Meister Eckhart's experience that "the eye with which I see God is the same eye with which God sees me." When we release our grasp on experience, we can then become several different subjects trading the experience within the same awareness.

The practice of mindfulness is facilitated by doing just one thing at a time without hurrying to get on to the next thing. California writer Sue Bender discovered this mindful aspect of work while canning peas with an Amish family with whom she was staying. She reflects:

> When we finished, we had forty jars of peas, each labeled and dated, to place in neat rows in the cellar. No one rushed. Each step was done with care. The women moved through the day unhurried. There was no rushing to finish so they could get on to the "important things." For them, it was all important. Which parts of today's process were a chore? Which were fun? There seemed to be no separation for them.... When I explained how split I was, loving to do certain things and hating to do others, the women laughed and tried to understand. "Making a batch of vegetable soup, it's not right for the carrot to say I taste better than the peas, or the pea to say I taste better than the cabbage. It takes all the vegetables to make a good soup!" Miriam said. No distinction was made between the sacred and the everyday. Their life was all one piece. It was all sacred—and all ordinary.[10]

If your job is such that you can't do one thing at a time in a casual manner, try attending to the general flow that is present, connecting the many busy tasks that make up the workday into a seamless loop.

Simplicity of Life-style. Many Americans value accumulation of more and more goods, upward social mobility and incessant activity as the only standard of worth. This attitude clutters up life with so many things that none of them can be adequately appreciated in their sacredness. A contemplative life-style aims at clearing away this clutter so the beauty of each thing and action can appear in all its glory. In his book *Voluntary Simplicity*, Duane Elgin writes:

> [S]implicity is essential for revealing the natural beauty of things. Rather than involving a denial of beauty, simplicity liberates the aesthetic sense by freeing things from artificial encumbrances.
> From a transcendental perspective, simplicity removes the obscuring clutter and discloses the spirit that infuses all things.[11]

In another passage, he uses a beautiful metaphor: "Simplicity allows the true character of our lives to show through—like stripping, sanding, and waxing a fine piece of wood that had long been painted over."[12] One needs only to think of the centered feeling one gets when viewing simple Shaker architecture and furniture to see the effects of removing clutter.

Simplicity also involves viewing the world as a whole instead of from the perspective of the grasping, limited ego-self. When one sees that others may be deprived by one's over-consumptive life-style, one becomes content with less. One way this has been expressed is in the admonition: "Live simply so that others may simply live." Meditation practice identifies one with the loving spacious silence instead of with the isolated ego-self and its possessions. This allows the contemplative to see that *all* beings—not just one's own bounded self—emerge with dignity and mystery out of the silence.

What are some ways of fostering a simple life-style? First, use time more wisely. Limit passive entertainment such as TV and radio to allow more time to appreciate the simple things of life such as a sunset, a loved one's facial expressions or the balance felt while going on a walk. Also, try to reduce the number of activities that you engage in. Pick a few causes that resonate within the depths of your heart and refuse the rest. Children especially need to be told that there will be a limit to the number of sports, clubs and social activities in which they can participate, especially since there is currently a tendency among young people to define their identities around being in as many activities as possible. Indeed, among the people I know, the most common obstacle to living the contemplative life is *busyness*. With conveniences like cellular phones, many opportunities for mindfulness are lost in favor of more busyness. This hectic pace has to be reduced for the contemplative to be able to contact the beauty present at the heart of things.

Simplicity can also be fostered by reducing material clutter in the home. In interior design, for example, concentrate on owning a few handcrafted items, rather than many cheaper factory-made items. An artisan can infuse more soul into a piece than a hurried factory machine operator can. Leave space around items to foster interior spaciousness and the ability to appreciate one thing at a time. Choose clothing and home decor styles that reflect personal, spiritual or symbolic values. For example, I wear Indian-made turquoise jewelry because it comes from a culture whose spiritual values I attempt to emulate, and because turquoise exemplifies for me the spacious sky-mind of meditation in which I seek always to live.

Finally, environmental simplicity encourages love for the natural world and for the food we eat. Eating low on the food chain fosters a wise and mindful use of energy. Recycling discourages excess stripping of the land. Gunilla Norris encourages us even to take out the trash mindfully: "I want to keep in mind the pine tree by the front door and how it keeps dropping its numberless needles—a tall and humble prayer. I want to shed my waste with quiet reverence like the pine."[13]

Relationship as Practice. In a society where commitment to relationship is often undervalued, it is important to view relating as a practice. Often the most beautiful spiritual fruits come after perseverance through the times of miscommunication that occur during the middle stages of relationship.

Contemplatives tend to be inner-directed and self-motivated. When they encounter rough waters, they often withdraw from others to work on solutions within the privacy of their own solitude. Spiritual community, however, is important for the growth of everyday contemplatives, especially those whose coworkers or even families seem uninterested in living a more spiritual life. Community can provide support and lift members out of stuck places. Christians experience Christ primarily in a spiritual community. I find that the warmth of Christ is revealed more intimately in community than in my solitude. The diffuse and mysterious glow of this presence is experienced in the mutual giving that occurs within the community. Of course, community does not have to be large: "For where two or three are gathered in my name, I am there among them" (Matthew 18:20).

A fruit of communal worship through waiting on God is the experience of what Quakers call "group mysticism." This is described beautifully by Quaker writer Thomas Kelly:

> In the practice of group worship on the basis of silence come special times when the electric hush and solemnity and depth of power steals over the worshipers. A blanket of divine covering comes over the room, a stillness that can be felt is over all. A quickening Presence pervades us, breaking down some part of the special privacy and isolation of our individual lives and blending our spirits within a superindividual Life and Power. Such gatherings I take to be cases of group mysticism. We may not know these our neighbors in any outwardly intimate sense, but we now know them, as it were, from within, and they know us in the same way...blended into the body of Christ.[14]

The depth of beauty of this divine blanket, however, occurs only in direct proportion to the degree to which the individual members are convinced of "the priesthood of all believers."

Another form of relational practice open to the everyday contemplative is the path of intimate relationship. Falling in love can be one of life's most spiritually transformative experiences. Often we are sexually attracted to a person whose personality traits are opposite to ours, and which we need to integrate into our own being if we are to become whole. Romantic attraction can provide a major portion of the energy needed to integrate these traits. Without it, we might not be motivated to follow through with the discipline needed to take on qualities that are not natively ours.

During the first few years of being in love, a couple's energy is focused on the relationship itself. But since sexual energy is at root spiritual, and since spiritual energy is by nature spacious and unlimited, the intensity of a mature relationship will eventually diffuse outward from itself. The love between the two becomes the energy needed to work on service-related activities focused on the outer world. Moreover, each of them will need to spend some time doing things alone and having other friendships if the sense of mystery so necessary for romance is to survive.

Anyone in an intimate relationship eventually experiences some disappointment and perhaps disillusionment. No partner can meet all one's personal needs. Facing the suffering caused by this disillusionment can draw both partners more deeply and profoundly into their inner wells.

A fruitful spiritual relationship can emerge when a man and woman find themselves in a friendship tinged with a romantic attraction that cannot be fully acted upon because of other relational commitments. This form of relationship was much written and sung about during the era of medieval courtly love, but is hardly ever discussed now. For the troubadours, not consummating the attraction ennobled one's character. Longing was transformed into the energy necessary for each to care selflessly for the other and to develop a love strong enough to endure the insecurity of the relationship.

Family life is still another relational discipline open to the everyday contemplative. A healthy homelife can provide a spiritual womb from which each family member finds the strength to go out and face life in a competitive world. The joys of child-rearing include increased opportunities to be mindful of the wonder of life. On the other hand, the trials of raising children allow opportunity for a parent to let go of expectations and to realize that children come not from us, but *through* us from the deeper source of unfathomable mystery.

I hope the principles and practices just outlined will ignite the reader's realization that everyday contemplation effectively opens up the sacred dimensions of the world around us. Meditation is not an escape from the world, but an immersion more fully *within* it. By identifying with both the spacious divine bliss that grounds the phenomenal world and with the flow of interconnectedness within it, the everyday contemplative can participate in creating a better world. Moreover, experience of the intersubjectivity of the human and natural worlds can lead to increased motivation to care for the world as part of one's self. Finally, meditative work with afflictive emotions and a life-style of simplicity can release the experience of deep peace within a stressful society. It remains for the reader to implement these principles and practices in his or her own unique way. We are indeed "a kingdom of priests!"

■ Notes

[1] Douglas Steere, ed. *Quaker Spirituality: Selected Writings* (New York: Paulist Press, 1984), pp. 12-14.

[2] John of the Cross, *The Collected Works of St. John of the Cross*, tr. K. Kavanaugh and O. Rodriguez (Washington, D.C.: Institute of Carmelite Studies, 1979), p. 316.

[3] Wayne Simsic, *Natural Prayer: Encountering God in Nature* (Mystic, Conn.: Twenty-Third Publications, 1991), p. 8.

[4] Simsic, p. 8.

[5] Simsic, p. 66.

[6] Gunilla Norris, *Being Home* (New York: Belltower, 1991), pp. 25-26.

[7] Rainer Maria Rilke, *Ahead of All Parting: The Selected Poetry and Prose of Rainer Maria Rilke*, ed. and tr. S. Mitchell (New York: Modern Library, 1995), p. 173.

[8] Dennis Genpo Merzel, *The Eye Never Sleeps* (Boston: Shambhala, 1991), p. 13.

[9] Richard Rohr, *Radical Grace* (Cincinnati, Ohio: St. Anthony Messenger Press, 1993), pp. 206-7.

[10] Sue Bender, *Plain and Simple* (New York: Harper Collins, 1989), pp. 48-51.

[11] Duane Elgin, *Voluntary Simplicity* (New York: Quill, 1993), pp. 30-31.

[12] Elgin, p. 146.

[13] Norris, pp. 27-28.

[14] Steere, pp. 312-13.

CHAPTER NINE

Lonely Valleys and Strange Islands: Contemplative Conversations With the 'Other'

by Mary Frohlich

> My beloved is the mountains
> and lonely wooded valleys,
> strange islands
> and resounding rivers,
> the whistling of love-stirring breezes....

These words from John of the Cross's *Spiritual Canticle* are a hauntingly beautiful evocation of contemplative experience. Yet just as watching an artfully prepared travelogue about the depths of the Amazon jungle is very different from being lost there, so actually to traverse the "lonely valleys and strange islands" of the contemplative journey often seems painfully different from reading about it. One soon discovers that the contemplative life is a sort of wilderness safari in which survival depends on rootedness in the wisdom of others who have lived it deeply and who have been given the charism of guiding others with their teachings.

In the past, most Christians who were drawn to a contemplative life sought and found initiation into an integral tradition that offered specific guidelines for every aspect of the journey. Yet today, many contemplative seekers find themselves without the benefit of such a single integral tradition. Meanwhile, we are presented with unprecedented breadth of access to an array of spiritual practices, movements and texts from both past and present. The increasingly accessible riches of our own Christian past would seem to provide an obvious source of nourishment for the aspiring Christian contemplative.

71

Yet many encounter serious obstacles to drawing on these classical expressions, finding in them attitudes toward such matters as embodiedness, sexuality, gender, sin, penance, authority and secularity that are profoundly at odds with the contemporary mentality. Thus, even if the seeker stays at home within the Christian tradition, he or she does not escape the experience of strangeness and even alienation.

At the same time, through written materials, tapes, traveling teachers and the Internet, the wisdom and practices of all the world's religions are knocking on our doors. Mixed in with these ancient traditions—and sometimes not clearly distinguishable from them—are hundreds of "new" spiritualities. Ecological spiritualities, bodywork practices, women's and men's spiritualities, along with the not-so-new practices of the occult such as astrology, crystals and psychic travel, beckon with promises of fresh and fulfilling approaches. It is a rare spiritual seeker today whose journey does not involve engagement with some or many of these spiritual expressions from beyond the orthodox Christian way.

All this is taking place within the context of the accelerating shift from modern to postmodern culture. Modernity was characterized by an optimistic belief in progress and in the possibility of rational—usually technological—solutions to all the world's ills. Postmodernity is characterized by the collapse of this optimism, accompanied by a radical destabilization of much of the normal human sense of rootedness in place, tradition and conviction. Faced with multiple and fragmenting religious options, some seekers may be blessed with finding a spiritual teacher from whom they can regularly receive individualized guidance. It is not unusual, however, to find oneself having to patch together the required wisdom by trial-and-error mining of a variety of traditions, texts and practices.

These times, then, are difficult and confusing ones for the contemplative seeker; yet, they are also rich with possibility. Thomas Merton spoke of contemplative transformation in terms of being freed from the machinations of the "false self" and letting the "true self" who lives with complete simplicity in God shine forth. No matter what the era or culture, the "false self" is always seeking to clothe itself with identity and prestige in terms of the standards of the world around it. The "true self," on the other hand, is naked, humble and without prestige; it has absolutely nothing except God's love.

A helpful metaphor for the life of the true self is that of "divine conversation." In this perspective we can view the contemplative journey as the gradual opening up of one's entire being to conversation with divine spirit in any and all circumstances. This conversation is not, however, a cozy chat on one's own home ground. Like Christ, who had nowhere to lay his head, we repeatedly find ourselves feeling dislocated, confused, even abandoned, as the context and language of the conversation shift around us. Over and over again, the Spirit refuses to settle down permanently in any of the tents we put up.

In this perspective, the great gift that the postmodern situation of fragmenting traditions offers—if one can bear it—is that it frequently and forcefully requires us to say goodbye to our favorite tents as we learn how to live as pilgrims, open to the foreign tongues, disorienting silences and radical demands of the divine conversation within which our true self is eternally being called into being.

■ CONVERSATION WITH THE 'OTHER'

In the journeys of contemporary contemplatives, fascinating and yet also troubling encounters with "otherness" are common. A few years ago I participated in a traditional Zen retreat of the Korean Kwam Um school during which we were trained in how to take our meals according to a highly stylized ancient ritual. The prayers and gestures preceding the meal, the number and arrangement of bowls and utensils, the foods and the way they were served, the procedures for eating and for cleaning up—every detail had meaning and was to be done "just so." Despite my best efforts to enter into the ritual, I remained mystified by much of what was being done. Nevertheless, the experience had a significant impact on me; I gained a kind of primal insight into the world of Korean Zen, in a way that would never have been possible simply from reading about Zen or even from just doing Zen meditation practice apart from its traditional context. Indeed, for some weeks afterward I was aware that the frame through which I viewed my everyday world had been shifted by that experience, in ways that were difficult to articulate and yet quite significant. The best I can say is that I was awakened to a dimension of ritual and rhythm and solemnity pervading and deeply grounding my being in the world. At the same time, many aspects of the experience still struck me as strange, antiquated and uncomfortable.

This is an example of how the "divine conversation" discussed above is not only an interior occurrence. Our God addresses us through the many "others" who shock us, fascinate us, seduce us, infuriate us or otherwise rattle our most cherished assumptions. Each encounter challenges us to discern the voice of God within it and to respond appropriately. Through these concrete interactions, in which our deepest personhood must both listen and speak, the character of who we are in the world is shaped and reshaped until only the simplicity of the true self remains.

Indeed, the notion of the basic character of the human person as a "conversational self" is a significant theme in contemporary philosophical and psychological thought. The model of the conversational self proposes that the self is fundamentally both internally centered *and* radically relational. The self, like a partner in conversation, has an interior point of view and at the same time is vulnerable to change in relation to those with whom it interacts. The conversational self is always in interaction and always changing, and yet it is not merely "knocked around" by events. The authenticity of the conversational self is marked by attentive openness to others' communications; by truthfulness, discernment and responsibility in one's communications to others; by the capacity for responsive change without forsaking one's own integrity. Here, the model of the conversational self is presented not simply as a theory for the sake of argument, but as the basis of some practical suggestions for how the contemporary religious seeker can interact authentically with traditions, texts and practices that derive from seemingly alien worlds.

In the above example, one could say I was "conversing" with the Zen ritual as I tried both to act with integrity within my preestablished perspective on the world, *and* to be open to engagement in the different values, hopes, assumptions and relationships that this meal-ritual embodies. Yet the difficulty and confusion that one often experiences in such encounters points to the need to enter into the conversation with greater conscious attention to how one is doing so. The remainder of this chapter explores the value of developing a repertoire of several different modes of approach to the spiritual "other."

■ ENTERING THE CONVERSATION

Conversations come in many varieties, ranging from uncommitted chit-chat to deep and long-term interactions that draw upon many different dimensions of our personhood. The approach I am proposing is more like the latter. Its assumption is that we desire to enter into the conversation with a "strange" spiritual tradition with a considerable degree of seriousness and commitment. This means giving the conversation enough time and enough focused attention to allow its real potential to unfold. The seriousness of our commitment, of course, includes the possibility that at some point we may recognize that it is time to withdraw from a conversation that is not bearing fruit or that is moving in a direction that we cannot in conscience follow.

As we move into the initial stages of the conversation, it is a good idea to do a bit of clarifying reflection on some basic questions.

- What is my primary identity as I enter this conversation? Am I coming as a disciple? A seeker? A scholar? A tourist? A challenger?
- To whom do I belong? What commitments, relationships, shared belief systems and so on shape the world from which I enter the conversation?
- Why am I in this conversation? What goals, desires, agendas do I bring to it?
- With whom am I in conversation? What commitments, relationships, shared belief systems, agendas and so on shape the other's world and way of speaking?

It is good to ask these questions at the beginning—and to come back to them from time to time as the conversation progresses. The conversation itself, if it is a deep one, will change our answers to each of these questions. We will most likely discover new, previously unheeded dimensions of our belonging, and we may even see shifts in our sense of who we belong to. We will surely learn much more about the world of the other—and in some cases, we will discover that our initial response to the question of "With whom am I in conversation?" often misconstrued the reality of our conversation partner.

For example, perhaps someone finds herself drawn to an engagement with the spirituality of Saint Francis of Assisi, a twelfth-century Umbrian (a region in what is now central Italy). Reflecting on the above questions, she notes that she is coming as a spiritual seeker (rather than as a scholar or a critic), that her own religious home has been shaped by the writings of Thomas Merton as well as those of contemporary feminists and ecologists, that she hopes to find nourishment for her own discovery of God in nature, and that what she knows about Saint Francis is that he wrote the "Canticle of the

Creatures" and that he lived joyfully and generously in relation to the natural world. Her main immediate access to Francis' spirituality is through an anthology of his writings that she has obtained from the public library.

After reading a few texts, including the "Admonitions" and some of Francis' letters, she realizes that the world he presents is more frequently concerned with issues such as devotion to the Eucharist, penitential practice and reverence for the clergy than with joy in nature. She also realizes more clearly how far she has moved from identification with these aspects of her own Roman Catholic roots. If she is going to pursue this conversation further, she will have to be open both to listening deeply to what Francis has to say about these topics *and* to doing her best to articulate responsibly her own questions and doubts about how this can be related to the aspects of Francis' spirituality that had originally attracted her. Indeed, a fruitful next step might well be to seek out others who have been engaged in this conversation for a longer time—present-day members of the religious communities that carry on Francis' heritage, for example. Yet even by having entered this far into the conversation, she has been changed— she has grown in awareness of the truth both of who she is and of who another is.

■ FOUR WAYS OF ENGAGING

There are actually a series of distinct stances from which we can enter such a conversation. Each in its own way can contribute something important to contemplative development. I would propose the following as four important ways in which we may converse with the spiritual "other":

1. We can enter the world of the other with reverence and the expectation of being taught, like a disciple.
2. We can seek to know the world of the other as objectively as possible.
3. We can resist and critique the world of the other.
4. We can "play with" the world of the other, creatively reinterpreting it and then letting it creatively reinterpret us as well.

Very often we will find ourselves naturally coming into a conversation from one of these positions, with little awareness of, or openness to, the alternative positions. Many of us have an ancestral tradition, a favorite saint or a special practice that we almost unconsciously approach from position one—reverence and an attitude of discipleship. For me, this is the Carmelite tradition of Saint Teresa of Avila and Saint John of the Cross. When I am preparing to teach an academic class, however, even if my topic is the Carmelites, I will most likely be leaning toward position two—understanding as objectively as possible. At other times I may approach a new practice or text with the adversarial attitude of position three—either because I am coming with a critical method in hand that I want to try out, or because I already know that it embodies something that offends my sense of value and propriety. Finally, when I am searching for a creative way to resolve a problem in my life or in the life of my ecclesial community, I may find myself naturally in position four—a playful and creative interaction with a spiritual expression as I let it open up new vistas of possibility for me.

Even though we typically find a "natural" stance in relation to spiritual traditions in one of these positions, we often create problems for ourselves when we make the assumption that this position is the only possible one. For example, perhaps I see the only available stance toward the desert fathers and mothers as one of discipleship. When I read in Athanasius's *Life of Antony* that after many efforts to tempt Antony the evil power henceforth presented himself "in the visage of a black boy," I may respond to this as a racist statement and regard my only options as either to repress my anger or to put the text aside in disgust. A stance of resistance and critique may indeed be needed, yet if once again I take that as the *only* appropriate stance I may never allow myself to glimpse the potential depth of spiritual wisdom that this great classic manifests. Use of contextualizing scholarship (position two), on the other hand, could help to explain the cultural genesis of Athanasius's image, while imaginative reflection (position four)—perhaps drawing upon the Jungian insight that the "shadow" or repressed dimension of a white person is often represented in dreams as a black person—could explore more positive meanings to balance the distasteful ones.

In short, we need the perspectives of all four positions if we are to engage fully in the conversation with spiritualities that are "other" in relation to ourselves. Let us, then, explore each of these positions more fully, and look at some examples of how they might enrich the living of a contemplative vocation.

Discipleship. In the first position, my primary identity as I approach the conversation is that of a disciple who belongs to (or wishes to belong to) the tradition or community of this spiritual expression. I come with a deep eagerness and openness to being formed by it. I believe that I can trust the world into which it invites me, and I allow myself to be vulnerable to it. The story above about the Zen meal ritual illustrates how deeply this kind of trusting participation can affect one, even when the tradition participated in is an "alien" one.

Closer to home, the ancient Christian practice of *lectio divina* ("holy reading") is an example of an approach to a spiritual text as a disciple. In *lectio* one reads slowly, attentively, prayerfully, pausing frequently to ponder and to enter deeply into the movements of mind and heart that are inspired by the text. One may spend an hour, or even many hours, with a single paragraph—just as one would joyfully "waste" time in attending to someone one loves deeply. In Christian tradition it is Scripture, above all, that deserves the time, trust and tenderness of *lectio*. It would be antithetical to this mode of prayer if one shifted into an analytical or critical mode. If questions do arise, one trustingly brings them to prayer rather than allowing them to distract one from one's singlehearted purpose of hearing the Lord speak through the text.

This reckless pouring out of the precious ointment of time, combined with a constant and singlehearted focus on the beloved, is profoundly countercultural in today's world of tight schedules and short attention spans. One who submits regularly to the discipline of such a conversation will find a deeper, more attentive, more gentle self being shaped by it.

An attitude of discipleship is obviously not appropriate if one does not have a sense of trust and an eagerness to be instructed by the given spiritual expression. On the other hand, in many cases it may be difficult even to gain an inkling of the potential that is present if one is not able to enter into this attitude at least tentatively. An example is a Western Christian approaching an icon—a core spiritual expression from Eastern Christianity. The natural tendency may be to regard the icon as "just a picture" or as on a par with other works of art with which one is familiar. Until one learns how to gaze with a deep openness and an expectation to "see the Lord," one remains uninitiated as to the true nature of the icon. No amount of study or reflection about the history, theology or artistic techniques of the icon can replace the insight gained from a single moment of experiencing the inflow of divine life in the presence of the icon—an experience unavailable unless one approaches with the reverence of a disciple.

The attitude of discipleship has traditionally been the stance of aspiring contemplatives toward the practices, teachings and texts of their own spiritual community. The difference in the postmodern context is that the seeker knows that discipleship is not the *only* necessary stance. The postmodern contemplative usually cannot rest in the position that Paul Ricoeur termed "first naiveté," in which the given account of the world is accepted without questioning. Ricoeur spoke of the possibility of eventually arriving at a chastened "second naiveté" that has faced and accepted the ambiguities introduced by critical scholarship. In view of this, let us explore some other stances for our conversations with spiritual expressions.

Contextualizing Scholarship. A second stance, typical of the modern world, is that of the student or scholar seeking knowledge about the historical and cultural setting of the spirituality one hopes to engage with. Here the "community" to which one belongs (whether explicitly or only implicitly) is that of the scholar. The goal of entering the conversation in this way is to understand the details of what is said and why it is said in relationship to scholarly knowledge of its context of origin. In doing this, one consciously moves away from the natural but naive tendency to interpret another's expression in terms of one's own worldview.

For example, sometimes Euroamericans who are attracted to Native American spirituality only perceive and affirm those aspects that correspond to needs within Euroamerican culture. These needs, which are valid in themselves, may include the desire to get closer to the natural world; to move at a slower and more sensitive pace; to be energized by communal rituals such as dancing, chanting, sharing the ceremonial pipe, or entering the sweat lodge. Many Euroamericans have enthusiastically embraced Native American spiritual teachers, but too often this is done while ignoring or misconstruing important dimensions of the cultural, historical and religious framework from which the Native Americans speak. At worst, this can result in serious distortion and exploitation of Native American culture and religion.

Let us look briefly at some of the influences that lie behind the proclamation of the Sioux prophet Lame Deer.

> Eighty years ago our people danced the Ghost Dance, singing and
> dancing until they dropped from exhaustion, swooning, fainting,
> seeing visions. They danced in this way to bring back their dead, to

bring back the buffalo. A prophet told them that through the power
of the Ghost Dance the earth would roll up like a carpet, with the
white man's works—the fences and the mining towns and their
whorehouses, the factories and the farms with their stinking, unnatural
animals, the railroads and the telegraph poles, the whole works. And
underneath this rolled-up white man's world we would find again
the flowering prairie, unspoiled, with its herds of buffalo and ante-
lope, its clouds of birds, belonging to everyone, enjoyed by all.

I guess it was not time for this to happen, but it is coming back, I
feel it warming my bones. Not the old Ghost Dance, not the rolling
up—but a new-old spirit, not only among Indians but among
whites and blacks, too, especially among young people.[1]

To fully appreciate Lame Deer's spirituality and the practices he rec-
ommends, it is helpful to know something about the nineteenth-century context of the original Ghost Dance, as well as about the present-
day context and promoters of his prophecies. Many aspects of the
Ghost Dance movement and its accompanying prophecies have
remarkable parallels in the responses of native peoples elsewhere in
the world to their invasion and oppression by technologically superior whites. One scholar notes that the nineteenth-century Native
American prophetic movements were "influenced by Euroamerican
models...including Christian biblical sources, missionaries, enthusi-
astic conversion, and the Great Awakening with its characteristic
apocalyptic and millennial expectations."[2] The original prophetic
movements were ethnocentric, intended to revitalize the Native peoples over against the whites. Today's prophets—including Lame
Deer—operate in a different context, however; important influences
on them include the New Age and ecology movements, and they
often are promoted by whites as much as by Native Americans.

Thus, scholarly study of history (political, economic and cultural
as well as religious), of the psychology of domination and oppression
and of cross-cultural patterns in religious experience can considerably change our perspective on what Lame Deer is saying. This kind
of information may not carry an immediate charge of spiritual excitement for us, but it is essential if we are going to enter an exchange
with him on the basis of reality rather than on the basis of romanti-
cized or prejudiced assumptions. This type of study by no means
needs to belittle Lame Deer's stature as a spiritual teacher; rather, it
is a necessary part of our allowing him to be a teacher for us. Rather
than conforming his words and practices to a comfortable shape
within *our* world, we can allow him to share with us the contours of

the world in which he actually lives.

One does not necessarily have to learn highly specialized scholarly methods and skills in order to relate to a spiritual expression in this way. In approaching written texts, the non-specialist can learn a great deal simply by practicing what is called "close reading." Close reading involves reading carefully and alertly, with specific questions and interests in mind. One notes any details or patterns that might be relevant to one's quest, as well as new questions that are stimulated by the reading. Often one returns to read certain sections a second or third time—not, as in *lectio divina*, to immerse oneself in their spiritual meaning, but to build up a clearer and more objective picture of the setting and meaning implied by the text. A similar method of close, alert observation in search of specific kinds of information or insight can be applied to nontextual aspects of spiritual traditions.

It is often remarkable how much can be learned from this sort of practice, even before making use of secondary literature. We can take as an example the following paragraph from Jerome's "Life of Marcella," in which he describes in detail the virtue and holiness of this great lay contemplative of the early fifth century.

> While Marcella was thus serving the Lord in holy tranquility, there arose in those provinces a tornado of heresy which threw everything into confusion.... Next came the scandalous version of Origen's book *On First Principles*, and that "fortunate" disciple who would have been indeed fortunate had he never fallen in with such a master.... You will say, what has this to do with the praises of Marcella? She it was who furnished witnesses first taught by them and then carried away by their heretical teaching. She it was who showed how large a number they had deceived and who brought up against them the impious books *On First Principles*, books which were passing from hand to hand after being "improved" by the hand of the scorpion. She it was lastly who called on the heretics in letter after letter to appear in their own defence. They did not indeed venture to come, for they were so conscience-stricken that they let the case go against them by default rather than face their accusers and be convicted by them. This glorious victory originated with Marcella, she was the source and cause of this great blessing. You who shared the honour with her know that I speak the truth. You know too that of many incidents I only mention a few, not to tire out the reader by a wearisome recapitulation. Were I to say more, ill-natured persons might fancy me, under the pretext of commending a woman's virtues, to be giving vent to my own rancour.[3]

Close reading of this passage provides us with a quite detailed picture of a major feud among early Christians. We learn that—at least
from Jerome's point of view—Jerome and Marcella were closely
allied, and that they were heatedly opposing proponents of Origen's
teachings. We glimpse the venom of Jerome's personality and the
intelligence and power of Marcella's. We hear veiled allusions to specific persons and incidents that we could undoubtedly track down in
secondary sources if we wanted to. We also gain some new questions:
What is the other side of this story? Why was this holy woman devot-
ing so much energy to this feud? What really was the character of her
relationship with Jerome, from her point of view? We could research
such questions, but even if we do not, they can open up many new
insights into Marcella's life as a lay contemplative struggling with the
cultural, political and theological currents of her own era.

On first glance this stance, with its home in the world of academia,
may not have such an obvious relevance to the contemplative quest.
In fact, however, the very alienness of the spiritual expressions one
encounters often demands that one enter upon at least a minimal
degree of this type of study. It is uncomfortable, and at times even
inauthentic, to take a stance of discipleship toward something that one
does not understand well. As questions of fact or meaning arise, the sin-
cere seeker wants to clarify the matter in order to know how to respond
appropriately. Movement back and forth between the stance of discipleship and the stance of contextualizing scholarship can be enriching to both, as insights emerge in each stance that can be explored
further in the other. It is important, however, to be aware of the distinct character of each, and—in Bernard Lonergan's astute phrase—
"to know what you are doing when you are doing it." Otherwise
one's scholarship may be mushy and one's discipleship shallow.

Critical Analysis. The need for yet another stance arises because there
are occasions when a spirituality comes across to us not as merely
puzzling, but as actually offensive. This third stance might be taken
by someone who belongs to (or stands in solidarity with) an
oppressed or marginalized element of humanity toward a work that
represents an oppressive majority. The goal of conversation from this
stance is to find a way to resist and reorient the oppressive implications of the expression. Often, when we find ourselves taking up this
stance unreflectively—that is, when we have an immediate "gut reaction" of anger, disgust or another negative emotion—our next move
is to reject or belittle the phenomenon that we are criticizing. Yet in

doing so we may lose the opportunity not only to have an impact on the other, but also to be enriched by what it does have to offer.

A reflective and methodical approach to critique typically involves applying a form of analysis that is not native to the world of the expression itself, so that its problematic hidden assumptions can be brought to light and criticized. An example is William Beers' detailed psychoanalytical interpretation of rituals of blood sacrifice in terms of male narcissistic needs to separate from and control women.[4] Beers works with this interpretation in relation to both Melanesian pig sacrifice and Episcopalian eucharistic sacrifice. The unveiling of psychological parallels between such diverse rituals— one very "foreign," the other quite familiar—can be unsettling, but it can also open up much-needed, realistically grounded reflection on the arduous and lengthy work that will be needed if we are ever to change such oppressive patterns.

As with the contextualization stance, there are many specialized approaches to critical analysis. Feminist, Jungian and liberation theology methods are all examples of approaches that have gained considerable popular appeal in recent years. Here is an example of an analysis of Teresa of Avila's writings that employs the methods of both feminist and rhetorical criticism.

> The assertion that Teresa "wrote like a woman" needs to be made with numerous qualifications. We can no longer accept notions of a "deliciously" feminine style, that is, the assumption that her linguistic patterns reflect an innate feminine mystique. Teresa consciously adopted, as a rhetorical strategy, linguistic features that were associated with women, in the sense that women's discourse coincided with the realm of low-prestige, nonpublic discourse. Teresa's feminine rhetoric was affiliative, but this does not mean that it was especially tender or delicate. Rather, by selectively adapting features from the language of subordinate groups, Teresa hoped to create a subversive discourse that was at once public and private, didactic and supportive, authoritarian and familiar. Her strategy was of necessity duplicitous. Teresa's rhetoric for women was an ironic rhetoric, used, first of all, to gain access to her audience and, secondly, to reinforce the bonds of a small interpretive community. As that community grew, Teresa proved that she was capable of modulating her strategy and her ironically feminine style.[5]

Once again, the question arises as to how such critical analysis can be related to growth as a contemplative. A contemplative seeks gentle openness to interior depth, whereas this approach is often aggressively analytical and oriented to an agenda of social and political change. It is certainly true that not all critical analysis is helpful for contemplative development. It can be, however, if the larger conversation within which the need for critical analysis arises is one that seeks to clear obstacles from the path of deeper openness to truth. Contemplative truth is not only God's presence in the depths of interior solitude; it is also God's presence in the poor and oppressed. Openness to the latter dimension of truth requires a desire to have the scales taken from our eyes so that we can see how the world's ways benefit some and impoverish others. Critical analysis aims to do this systematically, so that a way can eventually be found to remedy the injustice.

Imaginative Reflection. The fourth stance illustrated here is in some ways the most free. It involves entering the conversation with a kind of playful and yet practical attitude that seeks to discover a fresh, creative way of being and acting. Whereas each of the other three stances discussed here places the main focus on attending to the world of the other—whether by entering it, understanding it or criticizing it—in this stance the main focus is on giving the other a place in one's own world.

Some aspects of what is today called "theological reflection" have something in common with this approach. In relation to contemplative formation, theological reflection may be especially appropriate for those who have ministering roles—perhaps teaching or leading others in contemplative practice—and who want to discover the creative and empowering potential of a given spiritual expression for the community. There are a variety of methods of theological reflection that have been developed for use by pastoral ministers. A typical approach is that spelled out by Patricia O'Connell Killen and John De Beer in their book, *The Art of Theological Reflection.* They suggest four steps:

1. Focus on some aspect of experience.
2. Describe that experience to identify the heart of the matter. (Often the "heart of the matter" can be summed up in a rich image.)
3. Explore the heart of the matter in conversation with the wisdom of the Christian heritage.
4. Identify from this conversation new truths and meanings for living.[6]

In approaching an unfamiliar spiritual tradition or practice through this method of theological reflection, one begins by attending closely to the experience that is stirred up by one's initial contact. One looks especially for a catalyzing image that seems to express the central character of the experience. This image leads into reflection on related themes from theology or from spiritual traditions that are more familiar. When this reflection stage is culminating, one searches for the implications in terms of changed beliefs and behaviors.

For example, a Christian encountering the practice called "Transformational Breathing" is led through a series of relaxation and breathing exercises until he enters a balmy state of blissful feelings. Bringing this experience to theological reflection, he searches for a catalyzing image. Perhaps the words that seem to him to capture the gentleness, coolness and sacredness of his experience are "holy breezes." Moving on to dialogue with Christian theology and spirituality, he reflects on the biblical imagery of breath and wind, and is especially struck by the story from 1 Kings 19 where Elijah hears God's call in a gentle breeze. He does some reading on the theology of the Holy Spirit and on the mutual indwelling of God and the human soul. The culmination of the process for him is a rather subtle shift in his way of envisioning God's presence to him: God breathes from deep within, rather than simply being close by. The transformational breathing method, which is not in itself a Christian practice, is integrated into his Christian spirituality.

An important reason for placing this stance last is that it can easily be a temptation for contemporary people to begin *and* end here, in a rather light and free appropriation of the "other" according to the needs of the moment. Yet there can also be a poignant seriousness about conversation in this mode. Perhaps it is best to end this section by offering a poem by the Sufi poet Rumi—a playful poem that will surely make a home for itself in each reader's world in a different way, and yet may indeed have a profound impact.

The Many Wines

God has given us a dark wine so potent that,
drinking it, we leave the two worlds.
God has put into the form of hashish a power
to deliver the taster from self-consciousness.
God has made sleep so
that it erases every thought.
God made Majnun love Layla so much that

just her dog would cause confusion in him.
There are thousands of wines
that can take over our minds.
Don't think all ecstasies
are the same!
Jesus was lost in his love for God.
His donkey was drunk with barley.
Drink from the presence of saints,
not from those other jars.
Every object, every being
is a jar full of delight.
Be a connoisseur,
and taste with caution.
Any wine will get you high.
Judge like a king, and choose the purest,
the ones unadulterated with fear,
or some urgency about "what's needed."
Drink the wine that moves you
as a camel moves when it's been untied,
and is just ambling about.[7]

■ CONCLUSION

On one level, it is in poems such as those that begin and conclude this reflection that we find the most profound guidance for the contemplative journey. John of the Cross and Rumi traveled the whole distance of this way; they can speak with authority on its farther reaches. Yet as they remind us, no matter how well prepared we are we will nevertheless sometimes find ourselves lost in a lonely valley, abandoned on a strange island or drunk on a confusing wine, with none of our maps or strategies seeming to be of any assistance.

In such times, we learn in ever-deeper ways how true it is that for the contemplative, the stance of discipleship remains the primary one. It is there above all that one cultivates the interior depth of openness within which the springs of God's life will eventually flow in abundance. In times of lostness and desolation, there is often little that can be done except to affirm one's faith in the Divine Teacher and to trudge forward in emptiness and hope.

Yet discipleship can never be directed only to the transcendent

God; it also must have a human face. Within the contemporary context, the question of how, when and with whom to open oneself trustingly to discipleship is often complex. Living the contemplative life within the circumstances of the postmodern world—especially outside of a monastic context—will require of us the ability to know how and when to employ each of the four stances discussed here, and others as well. Contemplative discipleship lived in the midst of, and on behalf of, the whole created world's painful struggle toward the reign of God necessarily is that of Ricoeur's "second naiveté," in which one returns to radical openness and teachability having fully integrated the exercise of one's human capacity to understand, to criticize and to act.

■ NOTES

[1] Lame Deer, John Fire, and Richard Erdoes, *Lame Deer: Seeker of Visions* (New York: Pocket Books, 1972), pp. 112-113.

[2] Willard Johnson, "Contemporary Native American Prophecy in Historical Perspective," *JAAR* 64 (1996), p. 583.

[3] Ross S. Kraemer, *Maenads, Martyrs, Matrons, Monastics: A Sourcebook on Women's Religions in the Greco-Roman World* (Philadelphia: Fortress, 1988), pp. 184-5.

[4] William Beers, *Women and Sacrifice: Male Narcissism and the Psychology of Religion* (Detroit, Mich.: Wayne State University Press, 1992).

[5] Alison Weber, *Teresa of Avila and the Rhetoric of Femininity* (Princeton University Press, 1990), pp. 96-97.

[6] Patricia O'Connell Killen and John De Beer, *The Art of Theological Reflection* (New York: Crossroad, 1994), pp. 68-69.

[7] *The Essential Rumi*, tr. Coleman Barks with John Moyne (San Francisco: HarperSanFrancisco, 1995), p. 6.

CHAPTER TEN

Guidelines for Discernment of Lay Contemplative Formation Programs

by Wendy M. Wright

In third-century Rome the wealthy widow Paula, inspired by the teaching of Christendom's most famous scholar-ascetic, Jerome, determined that she was called to the contemplative life. After several years of practicing "house asceticism" with like-minded Roman matrons, Paula set off for the Holy Land. She took with her one daughter who, like her mother, was to vow herself to chastity and a life of communal prayer and penance. Paula had recently buried another daughter, a victim of ascetic zealotry whose fasting had become self-starvation. One child, a little boy, she left in Rome in the care of relatives. As the boat bearing his mother and sister sailed eastward to the far-off land of Christianity's beginnings, the little boy stood on the quay and said his last, tearful goodbye.

For a variety of complex reasons, Christians of earlier centuries held that the contemplative life must necessarily be a life of radical withdrawal. The story of Paula and her children illustrates this early Christian conviction that to practice contemplative prayer one had to abandon home and family, join a monastic community, take up a hermit's staff or enter an anchorhold. Contemplation was the charism, or gift, of a few—the spiritual elites—called to a life removed from "the world."

Contemplation today is still a call that some Christians come to feel is particularly their own. It is still conceived as a charism, a gift, whose cultivation is meant not simply for personal enhancement, but for the flourishing of the whole body of Christ. It is one of many gifts bestowed by the Spirit. Today, however, we prefer not to rank the various gifts as "higher" or "lower," but rather to see each of the gifts bestowed by the Spirit of God as contributing to the mutual building up of the body. For this and many other reasons, we no longer want to equate the contemplative life with monastic withdrawal.

In this essay my goal is to offer some assistance to those who do not live in monasteries, but who nonetheless are beginning to discover in themselves some inklings of this contemplative charism. After some exploration of what contemplation is, I will reflect on how one might discern whether this is indeed one's calling. Then I will look at the question of why one might seek something called "formation" in relation to this calling. In the latter part of the chapter I will focus explicitly on the use of discernment in making choices about specific formation programs.

■ WHAT IS CONTEMPLATION?

What is the gift, the call, of contemplation? How does one discern or distinguish the movement, the texture, the dynamic of such a call? How does one go about nurturing that gift? It will be helpful to begin with a quick overview of the history of Christian understanding of contemplation.

Through much of the patristic and medieval eras, contemplation was a term rather broadly employed. Gregory the Great, Augustine of Hippo and Bernard of Clairvaux, among others, used it to refer to a simplified, holistic way of approaching reality. In this understanding contemplation is a way that tends to wordlessness and the unification of thought, feeling and desire so that the energies of the whole person are gathered into focus in an attentive, waiting awareness.

The discipline of prayer that most typically embodied this contemplative approach during the first millennium, when monasticism was the predominant Christian spirituality, was *lectio divina*, "divine reading." *Lectio* involves the cultivation of a distinctive sort of listening awareness that probes to the point where the complexity and cacophony of reality gives way to simple silence, and time's relentless activity yields to the stillness of God. In *lectio* one becomes a receptive vessel, allowing the word to enter and transform one.

While still retaining something of this holistic meaning, over the centuries the term contemplation took on narrower, more highly defined connotations. Contemplation came to be divided into two phases, "acquired" and "infused," the first of these referring to the type of nondiscursive interior prayer that can be actively cultivated. Infused contemplation, on the other hand, was seen as a type of nondiscursive interior prayer that is a supernatural gift of grace, beyond the initiation or control of the one who prays. This approach was most clearly articulated during the sixteenth century by the Spanish mystics Teresa of Avila and John of the Cross.

Implicit in this definition was the idea that contemplation, in either of its forms, is primarily the work of those who live an ascetic life withdrawn from "the world." Implied, too, was a hierarchy of those who prayed. All leading the canonically established contemplative life were closer to God than those not leading that life. Those granted the special favors of infused contemplation were closer still. This Carmelite-inspired notion of contemplation dominated the Catholic world up until Vatican II. Most of the influential writers and scholars of the spiritual life accepted it as normative.

Since Vatican II there has been a return to the older, more holistic concept of contemplation, with the difference that now we no longer assume that contemplative living occurs solely or even primarily within cloister walls or in the solitude of a desert hermitage. While these venues retain their significance because articulate spokespersons for the contemplative life continue to speak from them, it is not true that they exhaust the possible ways in which a contemplative life may be pursued.

Contemplation in the present era is conceived both as a specific practice of nondiscursive interior prayer and, more broadly, as an approach to life born out of a cultivated contemplative attitude. Some of the specific practices are culled from the ancient Christian tradition. Centering Prayer, for example, is an adaption of the practice outlined in the fourteenth-century English classic *The Cloud of Unknowing*. A contemplative approach to life may issue from many different specific practices, but it is not limited to them. The contemplative approach orients to reality not as a problem to be solved, analyzed or manipulated but as mystery that elicits our reverence, claims our deepest desires and calls forth responsive love. It is a dynamic approach that teases us into transformation and asks us to be remade over and over so that we might image more closely the God in whose image we were made.

Essential to the process of remaking is the cultivation of an interior spaciousness. "Becoming a vessel" one might call it, or "emptying oneself," or "creating an inner cell," so that one may be filled and changed by God. Such a spaciousness has often been described by the quality of listening that goes on there—a listening that is responsive, receptive, integrative. Perhaps one of the distinctive characteristics of such an orientation is that, without ignoring the essential role played by human agency, the emphasis is upon divine agency acting, prompting and transforming. As we shall see, this attitude of listening and openness in readiness to respond to God is the foundation of any process of discernment.

People who feel drawn to a contemplative approach frequently find themselves called to specific locales that encourage that inner, responsive, listening spaciousness—monasteries, desert landscapes, retreat centers and the like. They go there not simply because they are attracted by an exciting program offering or in the hope of finding a community of like-minded individuals. Rather, they go because they are aware of a central, inner space that aches to be emptied out and freed from the noisy clutter that diverts attention from what Blaise Pascal is said to have described as "the God-shaped hollow in each of us that only God can fill." Often it is during such a time of deep, yearning listening that one begins seriously to consider the question of a contemplative vocation.

■ DO I HAVE A CONTEMPLATIVE CALLING?

The call to intentionally cultivate a more contemplative life comes from persistent inner prompting. One cannot take up this path simply because a neighbor, a spiritual friend, a present-day holy person or a long-ago saint has done it. Quite simply, some are called on this way. Others may find another path of intentional Christian living more fruitful. This is not to reassert the old elite mentality that used to surround contemplation, but to suggest that many other ways of Christian prayer and life are viable. They, too, are gifts, charisms, bestowed by God for the building up of the entire body. Immersion in activities designed to promote social justice, engagement in faith-sharing groups, parish ministry, devotional practices (such as the rosary), art or music pursued as prayer, theological investigations, recitation of the daily office—these and a thousand other paths are ways to follow the prompting of God's Spirit.

In terms of prayer, there are likewise a multitude of paths. Prayer may be conversational, imaginative, meditative, kinesthetic, vocal, liturgical, ritual, petitionary, visual, intercessory, short and spontaneous, formal and time intensive, and so forth. Individuals may have a general predisposition toward a particular style or practice of prayer, or they may find themselves drawn to different forms at different periods of their lives. In short, the contemplative path is one among many and may not be for everyone. Yet neither is it necessarily the special reserve of only certain "holy persons." What is more, one following that path does not necessarily eschew all other prayer forms.

What is most important is to pay attention to your own faith story. How have you met God in the course of your life? How have you prayed in the past? How do you feel drawn to pray at the present time? In other words, where is the Spirit leading *you*? Especially, how have you been gradually led over the last few months or years? You may discover that you are being called in the direction of a more distinctly contemplative path and desire to nurture it. Or that the prayer you have been practicing is basically contemplative. Or that you yearn for a network of support on the contemplative path you have long been practicing. Or that you desire to go deeper and more surely into the hidden ground of love and are searching for guides to accompany you. Any of these may be signs that a more wholehearted commitment to the contemplative path is being asked of you at this time in your life.

At the same time, it is also essential to be clear-eyed about the larger context of your life. On a practical level, what do you need at the present time? And what is possible given the context in which you find yourself? Do you feel an insistent need of several months or a year or two of intense immersion in contemplative practice? Do you need an approach that can be integrated more gradually and incrementally over a longer period of time? Realistically, how far and how often can you travel at the present? Do you have children, a spouse or aging parents to factor into your deliberations? What about integrating your contemplative practice into the work you are already doing, or into your life as it is presently structured?

Beyond reflection on the direction of your prayer and the context of your life, the initial discernment also requires some consideration of the issue of community and support. There is a certain solitariness about the contemplative path, whether that solitude is physical or not. Yet guidance, encouragement and support are essential. Contemplation is not about isolation or privatization. In a Christian context, contemplation is seen as a charism, a gift, called forth by a trinitarian God whose essential being is relational. The body of Christ, the Church, is an organic, dynamic communion of persons whose sharing of both gifts and vulnerability creates an interdependent spiritual whole. Individual contemplation in such a context is never simply for the sake of self-fulfillment or personal salvation. It is always, ultimately, for the community.

Thomas Merton spoke of the monk as the "marginal man" in the sense that the monk situated himself not only on the geographical margins of society, but on the hinterlands of the spiritual as well—in the wild, empty spaces where the ultimate questions come to constant birth. From there, a fresh perspective is possible, a transformed self can be forged. There is a sense in which Merton's claim is true for all embarked on the contemplative path, especially in terms of the solitary's relationship to the whole. Contemplative prayer brings into the whole community the awareness of the ground of love undergirding all reality. It probes the foundational empty openness of the human person. Thus the prayer of contemplation is not something a person does for his or her own perfection, actualization or enhancement. It is something into which one enters, with head covered and feet unshod. This most intimate, individual entering is at one and the same time an act of solidarity with and on behalf of the whole created world.

Ideally, such an act is undertaken with the support and encouragement of others. It is thus worth considering the concrete communal context in which you find yourself as you enter more deeply upon the contemplative journey. Are you in need of essential community support? If so, where can you find that? Frequent presence, shared celebration, the interweaving of lives—are these things you need? Or is your need more clearly to deepen or actualize a gift which you can then bring back to a strong, already-established network of spiritual support?

The texture and rhythm of your contemplative practice should ideally be suited to the situation in which you find yourself. While in some cases the Spirit may be prompting you to some radical change—changing employment, relocating, embracing a downwardly mobile lifestyle—in other cases a gentler adjustment may be asked. In either case, a contemplative life does not necessarily look the same in all persons. A retired, single woman may easily be able to structure a day to accommodate ample periods of seated meditation. A financially solvent pastor of a willing congregation may find that week- or month-long mini-sabbaticals at a distant retreat center are feasible. A young mother of several preschool-age children, on the other hand, may discover that scheduled times of reflection are impossible, but that a middle-of-the-night nursing session or prayers with a toddler before bedtime or pushing a stroller through the park are opportunities for a deep, unfettered attention to the whispered invitation of God.

Too frequently, Christians are convinced that they do not know how to pray or that they could never pursue a contemplative life, because they cannot imagine leading the sort of life they stereotypically assume is prayerful or contemplative. A married pastor with small children whose wife carries the bulk of the financial burden for the family, thus leaving him with much of the childcare, carpooling and household chores, reads *The Cloud of Unknowing* and becomes convinced that God is calling him to leave his family because that ancient manual (most likely written originally for hermits) insists that the contemplative life necessitates vast expanses of uninterrupted time in which "a cloud of forgetting" is cast between the prayer and the concerns of daily life. A working mother of five school-age children is dispirited because she attends a class on prayer given by a noted Jesuit author who insists that anyone serious about prayer must set aside an hour and a half for spiritual journaling each day at a fixed time. An older widow consults a spiritual director and confesses that she has "never known how to pray" because all the priests and nuns she has ever met have tried to instruct her in saying the rosary or doing a Forty Hours devotion— and all she can manage when she sits down before God is a wordless, joyfilled gratitude. A new wife and mother goes to a parish Bible study and asks some well-meaning women—some of whom are oblates in a Carmelite third order—about contemplative prayer. It is never suggested that she begin to pray out of the experience of holding her newborn in her arms; instead, she is told that the spiritual life requires radical detachment from all that is "of the flesh."

In sum, a genuine call to contemplation is an intimate personal invitation and will ask very different things of different people. While some may need to make a radical break with the past, others are called to develop a new contemplative awareness precisely in the context of life as it is presently configured. Even for the same person, the call will take different forms at different life stages.

■ WHY IS THERE A NEED FOR FORMATION?

The narratives found in the Book of Genesis assert that human beings were created in the divine image and likeness. The Christian community understands those same narratives to depict the prototypical human beings as "fallen" from their original state of created innocence. It is within the framework of this overarching story—of the intended grandeur of humanity, imaging God as it somehow does, and its failure to accurately reflect that grandeur—that Christians have for centuries devised practices and elaborated disciplines that can re-form humankind.

Various denominations have taken differing theological positions on how this re-forming might be accomplished and how much is dependent on divine initiative—or, indeed, whether such an enterprise is even possible. Be that as it may, for many in the Christian community, past and present, some sort of intentional shaping or formation has been seen as necessary in order for women and men to become what God intended them to be. That shaping has been understood as involving more than ethical or intellectual instruction. It has been conceived, to use the biblical metaphor, as making straight a pathway for God, as readying the person, both outer and inner, for the oncoming of the Spirit that will lead and inspire a life. For centuries, the "spiritual life" with its innumerable techniques of asceticism, devotion, prayer and good works, was seen in such a way: as the intentional effort to re-create a man or woman into the pristine divinized image that he or she potentially mirrors.

The history of Christian spirituality is littered with tales of scores of individuals and communities who took the notion of formation seriously. Desert hermits fled to the Egyptian and Palestinian deserts to be transformed in the forge of silence and solitude. Seekers flocked to monastic havens, "schools for the Lord's service," where under the discipline of obedience to the Rule they were refashioned in an image not of "this world." Devout believers went on pilgrimage, fasted, scourged themselves, engaged in countless forms of prayer and devotional activities, gave up sleep, chanted the psalms, became voluntarily poor, gazed on devotional images, fed the hungry, clothed the naked, visited the sick, worshiped, cultivated vision states, eschewed all action except an interior abandonment to God's will. The list is nearly endless. The point is that making room for, and then responding to, God's leading Spirit, however that is conceived, has been an impassioned pursuit since the inception of the Christian tradition.

In America today we have a somewhat more free-ranging conception of the spiritual life. Most people today tend to see the human person as intrinsically spiritual. To put it another way, we tend to see the whole person as composed of many dimensions: biological, psychological, intellectual and so forth. The spiritual is one of these. It is a dimension that requires a certain attention or nurturing in order for us to be whole—that is, to be what we potentially are able to be.

Whatever the philosophical or theological imperatives that prompt an individual to look for a formation program, common sense and observation on the state of the world are evidence enough that some new shaping needs to occur. The perspective that formation is a transformational process has certain implications, which may or may not be self-evident. First is that, although you may find yourself very interested, indeed fascinated or entranced with the notion of contemplative formation, it is probably safe to say that formation cannot be taken up in the same way as one engages in pleasurable recreational pastimes or hobbies that serve creative or entertainment needs. Second, it is not fair to expect a formation program to resolve problems—psychological, relational or otherwise. Finally, such a program is not best conceived as an attractive product—something to be purchased—of which one can avail oneself in today's open market of experiences, adventures and events.

Any program in contemplative formation is probably more accurately approached when its essential transformational character is acknowledged. It will require commitment, time, a willingness to embark on a venture whose outcome is not always clearly evident. Most importantly perhaps, a Christian contemplative formation program, while intensely personal, implies a community dimension. The call to contemplation, while sometimes solitary, never ends with the isolated self. The charism of contemplation is one of many Spirit-led gifts offered up for the entire Church, indeed for the entire world.

■ WHAT IS DISCERNMENT?

Seen in this wider context, the selection of a program is recognized as more than a personal choice. Instead, it is best to make such a selection by a conscious, intentional process of discernment. Discernment is a venerable practice in Christian history. Basically, it is the process of discriminating between the various "spirits" that seek to lead us. The classic discrimination is between the Spirit of God and the spirit of the "evil one." Today we might want to distinguish between various "voices"—both interior and exterior—that cry out for attention. What is the origin of a particular voice, perspective or consideration? Does it proceed from your own psychic baggage ("old tapes," negative patterns of thought, what "everyone else" thinks you should do, old fears, your "inner child," your compulsions and so forth)? Does it proceed from the prevailing collective opinion (only priests and nuns take courses in contemplative prayer; such courses are "flakey," self-indulgent, nonsense)? Does it proceed from positive self-interest? From clear-eyed, informed consideration? From a more diffuse, questionable source? From what seems to be God's prompting?

The point in discernment is to learn to pay attention to the various sources from which spring the many considerations that go into any decision. In other words, it is not merely a matter of problem-solving, of lining up the pros and cons and weighing them to see which side wins. Instead, attention to the texture and quality of the voices is necessary. One of the classic systems of Christian discernment, enunciated by Ignatius of Loyola in the sixteenth century, indicates that, at least for those already embarked on a journey toward God, the voice of God's Spirit will usually produce an affect or feeling of consolation, peace, certitude, joy, rightness, while the opposing spirit(s) will usually produce feelings of desolation, confusion, anxiety, dread. This greatly oversimplifies Ignatius, but it is not a bad general rule. Especially as observed over a fair length of time, consolation and desolation can be guides to identifying the inspirited voice of God amidst the chatter of the many voices that inform us. Not that affect is always unmixed; in fact, any discernment that comes with absolute unwavering clarity, fully formed out of the sky, is probably best allowed to rest for some length of time to see how it "wears." But in general, whether the overall effect of heeding the voice is consolation or desolation is a helpful guide.

Although discernment at its core involves this sort of inner attentiveness, it is nonetheless not an undertaking best done in isolation. We must also be attentive to the witness of Scripture, to the advice of trusted spiritual advisors, to the *sensus fidelium* (the collective sense of the faithful), to the best of ancient and contemporary thinking and the teachings of the cumulative Christian tradition, as well as to the concerns of those closest to us. Gather. Consider. Feel the texture. Assess the weight. Listen to overtones. Feel the quickening. Follow the deepest drawing of the heart. See where the plumb line falls.

It is helpful, too, to have some sense of the possible pitfalls that may confront one during any discernment. For some people, it is easy to confuse the longings of the heart with a tendency to seek spiritual highs. Constant intense consolation can be seductive, yet, tradition tells us, the spiritual life is not always a matter of intense, exciting experience. Some find themselves on a restless search for new spiritual excitement, moving from one technique or program to another, dissatisfied when the way becomes arid or routine. Unable to forge a more mature level of praxis on an established path, they are continually entering new ones.

Others may find that they are plagued by what the old manuals term "scrupulosity"—a sort of paralysis born of fear of imperfection or of being wrong, or a need to control every outcome. Perfectionism, a more familiar modern term, comes close to what the ancient term implies. A vital discernment requires, on the one hand, a vigorous confidence in our own power to discriminate authentically with the help of God's grace. And, on the other hand, a certain modest flexibility is needed—the gift to be able to modify or even give up our sense of the "right" discernment should new information or obstacles arise. Neither too timid about one's own capacities, nor too cynical about God's, nor too overinflated a belief that one knows the entirety of God's will: These are helpful qualities to cultivate when in a discerning mode.

■ WHAT QUESTIONS SHOULD I ASK ABOUT SPECIFIC PROGRAMS?

Not all programs in contemplative formation are the same. Nor do they all necessarily exist in the same universe of discourse. There are a few fundamental questions you will probably want to ask about the programs you are considering, beyond the obvious questions of program attractiveness, suitable location and affordable cost. Here are some considerations you might want to make.

Where does this particular program fit on a continuum of tradition and innovation? This is a question about both contemplative praxis and ecclesiastical style. Some programs teach prayer forms that are very traditional both in content and in language. Other programs may have roots in an ancient tradition but adapt its literature and instruction to twentieth-century psychology or religious diversity. Still other programs may be quite eclectic, borrowing elements from ancient Christian traditions and melding them with spiritual praxis from, say, Eastern religions. The late Jesuit Anthony de Mello's approach is a case in point.

Specific religious communities, even within the same family, may exist at both ends of a wide spectrum. For example, a program given by one house of a religious order may utilize primarily classic literature written by and for members of the order. The literature may use terms that assume a sharp division between the soul and the body, the contemplative and the world. It may assume a life of withdrawal or severe asceticism. Yet a program given by another house of the same religious order may be very different. It is important to ask the question: tradition versus innovation—to what are you drawn? What is right for you, in your present situation?

Community and solitude are on another continuum you will want to consider. In terms of the community dimension of a given program, you will want to consider how much shared praxis you find valuable or are able to engage in. A group that expects regular participation in the daily office or monthly meetings or ongoing covenant (faith-sharing) circles is different from a group that sponsors once-only workshops. Usually it is unrealistic to expect a program to offer the spiritual network that up until now life may not have provided. Nor is it fair to anticipate that a program will serve as a safe haven from a crumbling marriage, a disappointed religious vocation or a thwarted career. Rather, one needs a clear-eyed assessment of the state of one's network of spiritual support and a thoughtful consideration of the way in which any program undertaken enhances that network.

Does the program offer training that is essentially solitary? Does it intentionally promote community beyond initial formation? Does it offer instruction that you can carry back into your life away from the program? Or do you desire some ongoing commitment, a continuity of fellow travelers who will accompany you on your journey? Are you interested in a weekend workshop format or might you be called to a long-term relationship such as you will find in the third order or associate program that many religious orders—the Benedictines or Franciscans, for example—now offer?

One more continuum: freedom and discipline, both personal and communal. Some programs, as well as the specific practices they teach, are highly structured. They ask not only a high level of commitment (any genuine formation implies that) but a specific structured application. Intensive vipassana meditation assumes the availability of, as well as compatibility with, long periods of silent, seated meditation. Other programs may introduce practices that are more spontaneous or liable to individual interpretation.

A further consideration will be along the action-contemplation continuum. Although all of the formation programs described in this book are basically contemplative in orientation, they will differ in their assumptions about the life-styles that participants adopt, as well as in the extent to which they see contemplation as issuing in intense social involvement. Some programs will see contemplative prayer as primarily intercessory, others will appeal to those drawn to the hermit life, others will view contemplation as a necessary component in the struggle for justice and assume its members to be actively engaged in that struggle.

Alongside these continua—tradition-innovation, community-solitude, freedom-discipline and action-contemplation—will be the faith orientation of the program. This will overlap some with the tradition-innovation scale in the sense that certain programs will be led by and attract persons whose Christian faith is traditionally articulated, others by those comfortable with innovation and adaptation. These differences will no doubt revolve around many of the highly visible issues in religion today: for example, the role of women, the use of inclusive language, the nature of religious authority and so forth. While one would hope that any contemplative praxis would provide an arena in which differences of perspective on these issues might be transcended, nevertheless, programs, like people, have conceptual frameworks out of which they operate.

Again, one would hope that choice of a program would not be made solely along ideological lines, dividing Christian from Christian, nonetheless, one must have a certain compatibility with the worldview out of which a program emerges in order to be able to thrive and grow. For this reason, denominational and interfaith issues need attention in any discernment. While the sad divisions that segment Christian churches ought not to prevent interchange among Lutheran, Roman Catholic, Baptist, Eastern Orthodox or United Church of Christ, there are real theological orientations and "styles" of faith expression that mark us as Episcopalians, Presbyterians or Melkite Catholics. Formal or informal, emotionally expressive or restrained, silent or full of song, convinced of the reality of the dark powers or the incapacity of human initiative, assured that participation in sacramental ritual is sufficient, untroubled by any thought that evil might have an autonomy or that human beings might lack everything they need to know God fully in this life...the list is endless. The question is: Does a specific program allow you to integrate the denominational specificity you enjoy into your practice?

Similar questions must be asked about interfaith experiences. How does the program draw upon the wisdom of religious traditions other than Christianity? Does it teach yogic postures or sufi dancing or whatever? How are these integrated into your present faith orientation—or, if they are not, do you have the personal resources to do your own integration? Programs will differ in the extent to which they are exclusively Christian in their methods and assumptions, basically Christian but utilizing insights or methods from other traditions, or full-fledged interfaith experiments where the doctrine, metaphysics and worldviews of other traditions are taught along with particular contemplative methods. You will need to determine where you are called to situate yourself along the spectrum.

The same consideration should be given to programs that draw deeply upon the insights of some of the psychological disciplines. Transpersonal, Jungian, Depth—these and other schools of personal growth and development may or may not be woven tightly into the fabric of a formation program's working assumptions.

■ WHAT QUALITIES ARE NEEDED IN CONTEMPLATIVE GUIDES AND MENTORS?

A final reflection you will want to make is upon the backgrounds of the program's personnel. There is no easy way to judge the qualifications of instructors in contemplative praxis. But you might want to bear in mind two criteria: training and experience. Training may be certified—an instructor has completed a specified period of instruction at a given program and has been deemed to have successfully completed it and be qualified to instruct others. Or training may have taken place in the process of living a contemplative life, say, in monastic community. Yet neither certification nor contemplative affiliation is in itself a guarantee that an individual is a qualified spiritual guide.

Such a position of guidance is, in fact, a charism, a gift that is nurtured either through formal instruction or through long experiential trial and error. It is a charism that requires honing and fine tuning, but it is a charism nonetheless. In looking at any program, it is important to consider both the credentials (formal or "grandmothered") and the length of experience of the personnel. Have most on the staff been doing this for some time? Has the program a credible history? Does the staff seem concerned about questions of accountability (seeking supervision and updating themselves, or maintaining some internal system of evaluation)? Do they seem closed in on themselves or open to a constant evaluating of what they are doing and how they are doing it? Is humor and goodwill and a buoyant sense of life perceptible among those who staff and attend the program? Do faith, hope and love seem alive there?

A pitfall for some may come in the guise of charismatic spiritual leaders. An attractive, compelling personality may head a program or advocate a practice and individuals may find themselves seduced by personality rather than drawn by a genuine compatibility with the approach. Indeed, strong magnetic personalities abound in specialized spiritual communities. It is essential to be clear that the goal of any spiritual path is God, not fidelity to an instructor, adulation of a mentor or obedience to a guru. In the end, any viable program must bring a particular individual closer to God whether or not that program has or has not accomplished this for an admired acquaintance or a well-meaning friend.

Finally, especially with contemplative programs, it is helpful to examine both ourselves and our potential guides for any subtle or overt tendencies to elitism. As has been suggested, there are many gifts of prayer and ministry bestowed upon those in the Christian community. Contemplation is one of these. To teach or to study a contemplative way primarily because one considers it a higher or more advanced or more holy form of prayer is probably a risky business.

■ CONCLUSION

In the last analysis any discernment, whatever its complexity, is ultimately judged by its fruits. The Christian tradition names three especially: faith, hope and love. In the end, the discernment of a contemplative formation program is less like solving a mathematical equation or fitting together the pieces of a puzzle. It is more like the turning of a sunflower to the sun, the intuitive hunch of a scientist seeking a creative resolution for unexplainable, contradictory observations, the longing of a heart searching for a lost beloved, or the artistry of a musician, sculptor or choreographer delineating in sound, stone or the human body, the emergent, self-propellant, rightful line that says yes.

PART THREE

CENTERS FOR LAY CONTEMPLATIVE FORMATION

Introduction to the Site Research Project

by Virginia Manss

Preliminary research for this project began three years prior to the actual visits to research sites. The Association of Contemplative Sisters (ACS), acting as sponsors for the project, conducted a survey among its five hundred members, asking them to send names, addresses and other information on places of lay Christian contemplative formation with which they were acquainted through their own experience. As a result of the positive response to this survey, a list was compiled of one hundred and fifty places across the United States. A follow-up survey requesting more detailed information was then sent to those sites that seemed appropriate for further study.

Realizing that it would be impossible (and not even beneficial) to visit each of the sites recommended in the survey, a steering committee attempted to put some order into the list by categorizing the suggested places according to representative models. This categorization was simply to serve as an aid in selecting sites to visit so that the different and various approaches to lay Christian contemplative formation would be examined. As a result of its efforts, the steering committee created eleven different categories or representative models:

- Secular Orders/Associate Groups of Canonical Communities
- National/International Networks
- Communities with Formal and Informal Support Networks
- Retreats, Courses and Workshop Offerings
- Monastic Communities with Structured Live-ins
- Long-term Residential Opportunities
- Home Study Programs with Intensives

- Local Support Groups
- Ashrams
- Hermitages
- Houses of Prayer

An additional qualifying note: Many of the sites selected for a visit fell under more than one of these categories. The significant factor is that, of the sites visited by the research team, all of these models are represented at least once.

Many approaches to contemplative formation exist within the United States today. While this project aimed to be as broad-based as possible, the final product ended up being but a first step in mapping the landscape of lay Christian contemplative formation within this country. We hope this first step creates an invitation to others to etch out more of this landscape in the future.

The reader will also discover that the term "contemplative formation" has been used in its broadest sense in relation to this project. In this way we could include not only sites with structured formal programs, but also sites where contemplative seekers would informally come into contact with rich formative influences by way of their association with contemplative communities or by way of their immersion in intense silence and solitude.

Another objective of the study was to include research sites from a variety of Christian denominations. Twenty-one of the twenty-seven visitation sites have a Roman Catholic base, but whether this reflects the proportion of Catholic to other Christian contemplative formation sites in the country or merely the limitations of ACS's prior survey remains an open question. In any case, all but one of the sites visited were open to contemplative seekers of all denominations. Twenty-two of the sites are included here.

The research team began its work in January 1996. In one calendar year the team visited twenty-seven sites including networks, programs, houses of prayer, lay communities, monasteries and secular orders. The team interviewed founders and staff and entered into the rhythm of the programs as much as possible. Admittedly, their research offers but an introduction to, or a taste of, some of the programs and environments available for spiritual seekers looking to deepen the contemplative dimension of their lives.

As the year progressed it became increasingly apparent to the research team that their study could not be entirely objective or comprehensive. How does one, in one hour or one day or even three days, capture the rhythm and spirit of a place or program of prayer that has been in existence for twenty-five years? How does one, in a mere sliver of time, express the ebb and flow of seasonal prayer, of nature, of the qualities and experiences of those founders who embody the spirit of their life's work? In addition, the time limitations of the directors of sites as well as of the research team necessarily affected the fullness of observation. At some of the sites all three members of the team were able to be present; at quite a few places there were two members present; and at the remaining places, only one member could visit. This, in turn, affected the vision and breadth of each of the reports. Finally, all three members of the research team were Roman Catholic women, bringing with them their own limitations and biases (some of which were unconscious) and no doubt coloring their attempts at objectivity.

Having considered the limitations of an undertaking of this nature, it is beneficial to turn to the research members and discover what they learned from visiting so many sites of lay Christian contemplative formation. Some of their summary remarks from the experience follow:

- We learned so much during this year of journey and research. The beauty of the divine patterns at work through the men and women who founded these programs was powerful and awe-inspiring. A sense of timelessness and eternal, sacred unfolding emerged as we listened. God entered into the lives, vision and resultant practice in these places of contemplative space.

- We learned anew the wondrous physical beauty of this country of ours, from the deserts, to the mountains, to the cities or wooded forests. "Getting there" was as much a part of the sacred experience as "being there." In fact "getting there" was a part of the whole of "being there."

- We learned also that, although there are many programs available, there is still an untapped potential for ever new programs for lay contemplatives in the world, separate and distinct from adaptations of older historical monastic models. The lay contemplative, living in the "marketplace," not bonded by a physical center or support group, is still a relatively new phenomenon in the Church and world. We learned there is a need for new models and imaginative ideas.

- We learned, or relearned, that the contemplative stance, as echoed by the people and places visited, is countercultural, or perhaps transcultural. The physical settings, whether urban or rural, the interiors, the architectural exteriors (where applicable) were deliberately understated, uncluttered, natural, evoking an inner and outer harmony of place and interior being. The unspoken message was integrity and "less is more."

- Finally, we learned, to our surprise, how exuberant and excited both staff and guests and residents were at the many places we visited about our mission and project. Everyone we met felt uplifted because we were doing what we were doing. We drew strength and hope and gratitude from their enthusiasm about us. We felt like spiritual Johnny Appleseeds, not only planting seeds from place to place, but being given ever more seeds to plant.

All of the research collected here was created primarily as a resource for the contemplative seeker. As you read through its pages, it is our hope that you will discover places of nourishment and support for your own contemplative journey.

■ RESEARCH TEAM MEMBERS

Ginny Manss is a fifty-six-year-old laywoman who is presently a member of a small lay contemplative community. Ginny spent eighteen years as a member of a Roman Catholic religious order; twelve of those years were spent within a cloistered contemplative community. When her community disbanded in 1978, she continued her orientation toward contemplative living but this time within the context of the lay world. She intuitively recognized that new expressions of contemplative life were being realized within the lay world, expressions not yet marked by formal structures, but influenced by the influx of a greater Reality beyond form. Ginny affirmed her place within this movement as a lay contemplative. For several years she worked part-time as an assistant director of continuing education at the College of Mount St. Joseph in Cincinnati, Ohio. Later she became executive director of EarthConnection, a newly organized environmental educational organization. In 1991 she obtained her master's degree in theology from Xavier University. From 1992 to 1996 she balanced her contemplative lifestyle with a ministry of caring for the elderly in Green Valley, Arizona. Ginny has been a member of the Association of Contemplative Sisters since its founding in 1969. In 1992 she was elected president of the association, the first laywoman to hold that position.

Mary Bookser, S.C., is director of initial formation for the Sisters of Charity of Cincinnati. During several years as an adult counselor in the Women's Center of the College of Mount St. Joseph and instructor in Scripture studies and spirituality, she became more and more drawn to a contemplative mode of "sitting in the Center of the God Who sits in the center of her soul." Incorporated into her emerging spirituality has been a deep realization of the interconnectedness of all living beings in the universe and a growing awareness of the wealth of wisdom found in her own Catholic tradition, as well as spirituality emerging from the world's great religions. During her doctoral work in women's studies, literature and spirituality, she explored the similarities between some of the great women mystics and the shamanic experience. Her desire to live deeply aware of her connectedness to all life is enhanced by her choice to live in a simple passive solar dwelling on the Sisters of Charity motherhouse grounds.

Deborah Gephardt is a laywoman, sixty-two years of age, wife of a retired newspaper editor and mother of an adult son and daughter. She has been a member of the Roman Catholic Church for forty years. She is a college graduate, majoring in biology/pre-med and was a medical technologist before her marriage. The primary credential for her being included in this research team, she concludes, was her nearly lifelong attempt to comprehend and respond to the "Hound of Heaven," and her later search for spiritual teachers and guides to help validate and encourage the deepening contemplative orientation of her life. She struggled for years, and usually alone, to find teachers or programs that could help explain this new (to her) unitive, non-dualistic language that welled up from within and yet echoed the experience of the saints and mystics of all the great religious traditions throughout history. By trial and error, this search led to some of the programs reported in this research. In addition, she did some volunteer work in India as well as spending some time at the ashram of Father Bede Griffiths there. She is a member of the Association of Contemplative Sisters.

Lay Contemplative Formation Sites

by Virginia Manss, Mary Bookser, S.C.,
and Deborah A. Gephardt

■ CENTER FOR ACTION AND CONTEMPLATION

Address: P.O. Box 12464
Albuquerque, New Mexico 87195-2464

Phone: 505-242-9588

Fax: 505-242-9518

Type of Contemplative Formation Model: Retreats, courses, workshops

Founder: Father Richard Rohr, O.F.M.

Director: Kathleen O'Malley

Tradition: Christian, Roman Catholic, Franciscan in origin; also ecumenical

Sources: Christian theology and spirituality; Zen practice in daily communal prayer

Start-up Date: 1987

Participant Profile: Roman Catholic, but a good number from other Christian denominations participate as well. As of 1996, approximately four hundred and fifty had participated in the internship programs; thousands have been involved in retreats sponsored by the Center. Wide age range among participants; interns are in the range of twenty-five to seventy years of age. An equal percentage of men and women are engaged in the programs. Participants come to the Center for discernment, integration, growth.

Newsletter: *Radical Grace* currently has about six thousand subscribers in the United States plus circulation throughout twenty-five different countries.

Programs: Includes structured weekend programs with nationally recognized speakers, two- and six-week internships. Application process is required for six-week internships.

Cost (as of June, 1999): Weekend retreat (without lodging)—$130; Internships—6 weeks, $1,800; 2 weeks, $800. Partial scholarships are a possibility.

The Center for Action and Contemplation (CAC) is located in the western part of Albuquerque, New Mexico, in a distinctly Hispanic section of the city known as "the valley." While the urban character of this modern yet historical city is immediately apparent, a rural atmosphere is likewise noticeable in the neighborhood that directly engulfs CAC's guest residence, Tepeyac. Guests awaken each morning to the crow of roosters and can walk a short distance to view horses grazing in yards adjacent to the modest homes that comprise this section of the city.

The Center consists of two buildings: the Center itself, a long, low-slung building on the grounds of Holy Family Catholic Church, houses offices, a large community room, a chapel and a well-stocked library of books and tapes on peace and justice issues, spirituality, prayer and other related topics; the other building, less than a mile away from the Center, is the Tepeyac Guest House. Tepeyac, which is home to those making the CAC internships, is a big, southwestern-style, beamed-and-stucco house consisting of a large living room with fireplace, a roomy, comfortable kitchen and dining area, a small library and several guest sleeping quarters (as well as a small meditation chapel) branching off from the main house.

The site chosen for CAC is deliberately in keeping with the purposes of its founder, Rev. Richard Rohr. Those who come to the Center are seeking not an escape from engagement in social activism, but rather an integration of their action with contemplation. The location of the Center and its guest house in this multicultural city of over half a million people places the occasions for both action and contemplative prayer at participants' fingertips. The internship program in particular involves participants in volunteer work at local direct service agencies and in CAC's witness activities as well as in regularly scheduled times of contemplative prayer and silence in the Center's simple Zen-like prayer room.

Emphasis is placed upon the word *and* in the Center's title. As Father Richard Rohr suggests, "You can be an engaged apostolic person in the world and a contemplative." He explains further that "contemplation gives a reconstituted sense of the self (the vine and the branches imagery of Scripture)...and the thing that comes from it is the contemplative person doesn't need to fix or control everything... one lives out of that contemplative space choicefully, consciously."

The most comprehensive and intensive offering at the Center is the six-week internship program. The CAC accepts as interns those who desire an intensive spiritual formation process. The internship program includes:

1. Regularly scheduled times of contemplative and group prayer
2. Residence in Tepeyac and participation in the simple vegetarian life-style practiced there
3. Weekly one-on-one meetings with a CAC staff person or CAC representative
4. Participation in weekly group meetings to process ongoing internship experience
5. Participation in CAC gatherings such as workshops, classes, liturgical celebrations
6. Participation in major CAC programs taking place during the time of internship
7. Household responsibilities at Tepeyac
8. Volunteer time at a local direct-service agency
9. Participation in CAC's witness activities

The primary approach of the Center is experiential/reflective; the primary aim is integration. Though the bias of the Center is toward action, involvement, incarnation, CAC seeks to give Christian social activists a taste, perhaps a first taste, of contemplative prayer and tries to help participants ground their activism in contemplation. CAC offers and requires a commitment daily to this other side of action while, at the same time, providing the environment for community through the shared work and prayer of the participants. The Center's intention is far more difficult than that of its counterparts who are strictly devoted to developing the contemplative dimension of life or who are dedicated to social activism. The integration of the two dimensions is precisely the point of tension. Whether CAC can creatively reconcile the two dimensions remains to be seen.

FEATURES FOR DISCERNMENT

- Oriented heavily toward community and social action
- Emphasis on ecological sensitivity: vegetarian meals prepared by residents, recycling, permaculture
- Oriented toward the beginner in contemplative prayer
- Unique in its attempt to integrate the active and contemplative dimensions
- Semirural setting

SAMPLE SCHEDULE *(First week of Two-Week Internship Program)*

Monday

9:00-4:00	Arrival at Tepeyac
4:00	Program Orientation
6:00	Dinner for Interns and Staff
7:00	Intern/Staff Introductions

Tuesday

7:40-8:00	Contemplative Prayer
8:30	CAC Tour
9:30-11:00	Contemplative Prayer Seminar
1:30-1:50	Contemplative Prayer
2:15	Tepeyac Permaculture Orientation
6:00	Dinner

Wednesday

7:40-8:00	Contemplative Prayer
9:00-10:30	Group Process
11:00-12:30	Contemplative Prayer Seminar
1:30-1:50	Contemplative Prayer
2:30-4:00	Video: *The Day After Trinity* (optional)
6:00	Dinner
7:30-9:00	Presentation: Saints Francis and Clare

Thursday

7:40-8:00	Contemplative Prayer
	Leave for Border Awareness Experience, an immersion experience in communities along the border of Mexico and the United States, living with marginalized people in their homes for four days.

■ DESERT HOUSE OF PRAYER

Address: 7350 W. Picture Rocks Road
P.O. Box 570, Cortaro, Arizona 85652

Phone: 520-744-3825

Fax: 520-744-0774

Type of Contemplative Formation Model: Retreats, hermitage, house of prayer

Founder: Father John Kane, C.Ss.R.

Tradition: Christian, Roman Catholic

Sources: Contemplative tradition of Western and Eastern mystics, Thomas Merton, Jesus Prayer

Start-up Date: February 3, 1974

Participant Profile: Though the foundation of Desert House is Roman Catholic Christian, guests come from a wide range of Judeo-Christian backgrounds and some from various Eastern religions. Desert House serves men and women of all ages and faiths in all stages of contemplative growth.

Newsletter: *Exodus* is published bimonthly. Written by Father John Kane, the newsletter is distributed to associates and former retreatants at the house of prayer.

Programs: No formal programs are offered. People come to Desert House for periods of silence and solitude, for private retreats, for a desert experience. Their stay may last for a few days, a few weeks or longer if desired. Spiritual direction is available upon request.

Cost (as of June 1999):

    Rooms: $34 per day ($31 per day after 3 days)

    Hermitage: $39 per day ($34 per day after 3 days)

"I will lead you into the desert and there I will speak to your heart." These words of Isaiah, inscribed on the front wall of the chapel at nearby Picture Rocks Retreat Center, capture in a very real sense the origin, spirit and main work of Desert House of Prayer. Having been lured into the desert themselves, the core group (Father John Kane, C.Ss.R., Sister Louise Margaret Williams, C.PP.S., and Sister Dorothy Ann Lesher, C.S.J.) in the early 1970's set about to provide a house of prayer where others could find the solitude and silence not afforded them in their everyday lives. Over the years the staff has increased to six and the range of people coming to Desert House for brief or extended periods of time has grown to include pastors, parents, nuns, nurses, teachers, wives, husbands, doctors, lawyers, single people, students and others.

Originally an extension of the Redemptorists' Picture Rocks Retreat House, Desert House settled into its own sacred space in 1980 on a thirty-one-acre tract of land located directly across the road from the retreat center. Desert House would eventually be comprised of several buildings, all offering a simplicity in harmony with its purpose and surrounding environs. The community building houses a large common room with fireplace and dining area, a kitchen and office space. There are two separate guest buildings, each with six individual guest quarters; at a distance from the other buildings, there are four self-contained hermitages. Another building houses an impressive library with its collection of nearly ten thousand volumes and a special area devoted entirely to the works of Thomas Merton. A large chapel, with inviting views of the surrounding mountains, completes the network of buildings that comprise this house of prayer.

The buildings at Desert House open to the high desert country at the foot of Safford Peak (an ancient holy mountain) in the Tucson Mountains west of Tucson, Arizona. In spite of surrounding suburban sprawl in recent years, the house of prayer has maintained its environment of solitude, quiet and rich desert beauty.

A spirit of silence permeates the atmosphere of this house of prayer. It is not a forced quiet, but rather a quiet that seems to be spoken first by the desert and echoed in the spirits of the staff and guests. Sister Gabriel Herbers, a former administrator at Desert House, notes that people coming today, even younger people, "already understand contemplative life, have a greater understanding of the place of silence. Perhaps it is fueled by the pace of life today. They come to nurture and restore their spiritual life." She adds, "There is a greater need now than ever for a place of solitude. It is impossible to become an activist without first becoming a contemplative. From that stance one becomes an activist. Those who burn out have not developed that rhythm, this grounding in contemplation."

The way in which one spends time at Desert House is shaped by individual need. One may choose to participate in opportunities for common daily prayer. The Eucharist and Morning Prayer and Vespers are celebrated together daily as well as two periods of centering prayer. One may feely choose to forego any of the above and be immersed more completely in solitude.

While no formal programs are offered at Desert House as a rule, there is a Wednesday night forum that invites guests to study present-day peace and justice issues. This forum, facilitated by a social activist, Father Ricardo, is intended as an aid to awareness of the larger social issues in which each Christian is immersed and to counter the temptation of the person of prayer to retreat from the world and its concerns.

Guests will find at Desert House an emphasis on integration and development of the whole person. To this end, attention is paid to the fine arts, with many original works of art and photography on view, a good collection of classical music on CDs and the availability of fine literature. While other meals are taken in silence, a common meal at the end of each day enables guests to become acquainted with one another and also taste the community spirit of staff members.

FEATURES FOR DISCERNMENT

- Captivating desert setting
- Staff solidly anchored in spirituality and community
- Solid guidance for beginners; non-intrusive support for more advanced
- Creative balance between structure and freedom, solitude and community

SAMPLE SCHEDULE

Each day: Roman Catholic Eucharist, Liturgy of the Hours (Morning and Evening Prayer), centering prayer twice daily. Each retreatant is encouraged to engage for an extended time each day in the classical steps of prayer, *lectio* (serious reading), *meditatio* (reflection), *oratio* (praying with words), *contemplatio* (prayer without words).

Each week: For most of the year, from Saturday evening until Sunday morning, a night vigil is held before the Blessed Sacrament, at one-hour intervals.

Each month: A three-day retreat consisting of four hours of group centering prayer each day.

■ OUR LADY OF SOLITUDE CONTEMPLATIVE HOUSE OF PRAYER

Address: P.O. Box 1140
        Black Canyon City, Arizona 85324

Phone: 623-374-9204 (fax also)

Type of Contemplative Formation Model: Hermitage, house of prayer, long-term residential opportunities

Foundress: Sister M. Therese Sedlock, O.S.F.

Tradition: Christian, Roman Catholic, Franciscan, Carmelite, Cistercian

Sources: Scripture, Thomas Merton, John of the Cross

Start-up Date: 1980

Participant Profile: A fairly equal mix of men and women from Roman Catholic backgrounds as well as other Christian faiths come to Our Lady of Solitude for periods of intense silence, solitude and prayer. Married people, vowed religious, priests, single people, ranging in ages from the mid-twenties to the mid-seventies come to this contemplative house of prayer for contemplative-eremitical experience and living. Their average stay may be as short as three days or as long as a year.

Programs: Individual directed Scripture retreats of three to ten days, desert spirituality live-ins of two to five weeks, extended live-ins from a month to a year.

Cost (as of July 1999): Suggested per diem rate $25; $600 per month (over three months, $500 per month).

Some forty miles north of the hustle and bustle of Phoenix, Arizona, atop a high desert mesa overlooking Black Canyon City, sits a rather extraordinary place of contemplative prayer. Guests arriving at the gate at the base of the hill immediately encounter a very steep ascent leading to the main house at the top. About halfway up, on an adjacent knoll to the left, they can view a striking circular white meditation chapel and a string of four simple hermitages all offering panoramic views of the surrounding mountains. At the top of the hill, in its own solitary space, sits the main building, which offers retreat-ants a prayer room, a large sitting room with an imposing fireplace, a kitchen, a library with over fourteen hundred volumes.

Sister Therese Sedlock, O.S.F., foundress of Our Lady of Solitude (OLS), is quick to acknowledge that OLS is first and foremost a "way of life and not a business," and that its main reason for being is to foster the contemplative, eremitical (hermit) life. For this reason only a small number of guest-retreatants are accepted at one time.

What one can expect to find at this contemplative house of prayer is an environment where all is directed toward being alone with God. To ensure this deep solitude prayer experience, all activities are carried out in total silence. The only communal gathering is a daily communion service or Roman Catholic Mass in the meditation chapel. Even the liturgical celebration is kept simple and low-key in consonance with the one simple occupation of the contemplative.

The traditions out of which Our Lady of Solitude emerges are Catholic Christian, Franciscan, Carmelite and Cistercian. Although there is a well-stocked library on the classics of spirituality of many traditions, the primary orientation here, as may be expected, is experiential.

Our Lady of Solitude is authorized by and responsible to the Bishop of Phoenix. Remarkably, the contributions of benefactors have not only initiated this contemplative space in 1984 but sustained it over the years.

OLS offers the experience of deep solitude to persons in all stages of contemplative growth. A newcomer to contemplative prayer more than likely would find this plunge into greater solitude a bit overwhelming, especially if he or she stays for any length of time. Spiritual guidance is available upon request for those who feel a need for direction. An internship is also offered for anyone who feels called to a more prolonged stay.

FEATURES FOR DISCERNMENT

- Intense degree of solitude and silence
- Highly unstructured, only communal gathering is daily Catholic communion service
- One staff member
- Three available hermitages

■ CONTEMPLATIVE OUTREACH

Address: (International Headquarters)
      10 Park Place, P.O. Box 737
      Butler, New Jersey 07405

Phone: 973-838-3384

Fax: 973-492-5795

Type of Contemplative Formation Model: International network; local support groups; retreat, course and workshop offerings

Founder: Father Thomas Keating, O.C.S.O.

Executive Director: Gail Fitzpatrick-Hopler

Tradition: Christian, Roman Catholic

Sources: Teachings of Father Thomas Keating

Start-up Date: 1984

Participant Profile: Since its inception in 1984, Contemplative Outreach has expanded to the point where, as of July 1999, there were forty thousand people on the mailing list and three to four times that number of people involved in its practice of centering prayer. The network is Roman Catholic in its origins but ecumenical in scope. Approximately sixty-six percent of current practitioners are women, thirty-four percent are men. Practitioners' ages range from twenty-eight to eighty-five years. Contemplative Outreach attracts people from all walks of life, single people, married, divorced, religious, clergy. The network offers programs for beginners as well as those more advanced in centering prayer.

Newsletter: *Contemplative Outreach* is published by volunteer help through the international headquarters and informs members in the network of upcoming retreats, workshops and other related events scheduled across the country. The newsletter is offered to anyone who has attended an "Introduction to Centering Prayer" workshop.

Internet: *http://www.contemplativeoutreach.org.*

Programs: Programs include Introductory Centering Prayer workshops and retreats, Intensive and Advanced Centering Prayer retreats and Formation Training for group leaders.

Cost: Program cost varies according to type and length of program as well as location.

Formed in 1984, the Contemplative Outreach network has experienced enormous growth within its fifteen years of existence. Its reason for being is to "introduce people to contemplative prayer in the Christian tradition and to provide a support system to sustain their spiritual development."

From its origins to the present, Father Thomas Keating, a Trappist monk of St. Benedict's Abbey in Snowmass, Colorado, has been the animating presence of the movement. With his many books, audiotapes and videotapes on contemplative prayer, and centering prayer in particular, Father Keating has provided the spiritual and conceptual support underlying the network.

Gail Fitzpatrick-Hopler, executive director, explains that Contemplative Outreach is a "bottoms up organization." Programs and workshops are created in response to what people want and need. Intensive retreats, post-intensive retreats, formation training workshops were developed to deepen the already established practice of those who had attended the initial centering prayer workshops. Centering prayer support groups were organized across the country and assisted by the national office in response to those who were wanting a means of sustaining spiritual development after they returned home from attending an initial centering prayer workshop. A telephone support line at the international office was set up to offer nonprofessional spiritual counseling to those engaged in the daily practice of centering prayer. The *Contemplative Outreach News* keeps readers informed of upcoming retreats, workshops, teleconferences as well as of activities within the various support groups around the country. Informative articles by Father Keating and others serve an educational as well as inspirational purpose.

Gail attributes the enormous growth of and response to Contemplative Outreach's programs to people's search for a deeper relationship with God. Encouraged to practice centering prayer with two twenty-minute periods per day, people experience the enormous power of silence; they taste the love from others sitting together in silent prayer. This kind of prayer has a transformative effect upon the individual that overflows into their daily lives and society at large.

While programs of Contemplative Outreach are conducted in various areas around the country, many of its workshops and retreats are held at St. Benedict's Retreat Center in Snowmass, Colorado. The monastery and Retreat Center are located beneath the Colorado Rockies' Elk Range at an elevation of eight thousand feet and approximately twenty miles from Aspen, Colorado. The retreat center, located about five minutes away from the monastery, has eight self-contained units with kitchenettes and baths. Adjoining buildings house a chapel/ meditation hall, conference room, kitchen, dining room and library.

A third branch of Contemplative Outreach was Chrysalis House, a retreat center in Warwick, New York, which provided a live-in contemplative experience for its core community and others who came for brief or extended stays. After ten years of existence, Chrysalis House permanently closed its doors in May 1996.

Contemplative Outreach continues to be a vibrant network of contemplative men and women whose enormous growth gives testimony to the widespread hunger among the laity to develop and nurture their contemplative dimension. The overwhelming success of this network may be attributed, in large part, to what is contained within its own self-description; it is a "network of faith communities, Catholic in origin, ecumenical in scope, committed to renewing the contemplative dimension of the Gospel in everyday life." Its teaching on centering prayer and *lectio divina* (a prayerful, reflective listening to scriptural texts) has provided the laity with a method and a practice applicable to everyday life that facilitates the development of contemplative prayer.

FEATURES FOR DISCERNMENT

- Primarily a grass roots network
- Graduated programs for different stages of progression
- Structured local support groups for ongoing development
- Emphasis upon a sustained daily practice
- Ongoing participation in broad community

■ SUMMER SEMINAR ON CARMELITE SPIRITUALITY

Location: St. Mary's College
  Notre Dame, Indiana 46556-5001

Sponsor: Center for Spirituality, St. Mary's College

Phone: 219-284-4636

Fax: Center for Spirituality 219-284-4716; Carmelite Institute 202-635-3538

Type of Contemplative Formation Model: Retreats, courses, workshops

Carmelite Forum: Donald Buggert, O.Carm.; Kevin Culligan, O.C.D.; Keith J. Egan, T.O.Carm.; Constance FitzGerald, O.C.D.; Kieran Kavanaugh, O.C.D.; Ernest E. Larkin, O.Carm.; Steven Payne, O.C.D.; Vilma Seelaus, O.C.D.; John Welch, O.Carm.

Tradition: Christian, Roman Catholic, Carmelite

Sources: Teresa of Avila, John of the Cross, Therese of Lisieux and others

Participant Profile: Participants attending the seminar are Christians from Roman Catholic, Protestant and Evangelical denominations. Usually women comprise around two-thirds of the participants, but some seminars have approximately fifty percent men and fifty percent women. Priests, religious, ministers, married (some couples) and single people have all participated in the seminar. Participants are generally over thirty-five or forty, with a few younger people ordinarily attending as well.

Internet: *http://www.carmeliteinstitute.org*

Cost (as of June 1998): $420 includes room, board and tuition

In 1996 the Tenth Annual Summer Seminar on Carmelite Spirituality was held at St. Mary's College, Notre Dame, Indiana. The week-long seminars are offered by the Carmelite Forum, a group of eight well-known Carmelite spiritual teachers, historians and authors. The Carmelite Forum was organized in 1982, honoring the fourth centenary of the death of Saint Teresa of Avila. As Sister Constance FitzGerald said, "The summer seminar is one of the things we do. The purpose of the Forum is to try to bring Carmelite spirituality into the American Church, into the midst of people, to make it available to people at large. The summer seminar is a wonderful way of effecting that."

The summer seminars attract one hundred and fifty to one hundred and sixty people each year, both lay and religious, men and women. Some have returned year after year.

The goal of the 1996 seminar was to "offer an experience of Carmelite Spirituality and to examine the life and writings of Saint Therese of Lisieux as a way of helping those who wish[ed] during 1997 to participate more fully in the hundredth anniversary of the death of St. Therese." Solitude, common prayer, daily Eucharist, reading sessions, workshops, lectures and discussions constituted the days of this one-week seminar.

Each day there was a large-group formal lecture by one of the members of the Carmelite Forum. Later in the mornings were seven smaller reading sessions, each moderated by one of the presenters. Each group studied and shared the same sections of texts, in this case, the writings of Therese of Lisieux. Participants could choose whatever moderator or facilitator they preferred. After lunch there was time for study or solitude; then there were two sets of workshops offered by the members of the Forum. These were ongoing, continuing one theme throughout the week. There were workshops on Spiritual Guidance, God in the Human Story, Program of Life, Experience of Darkness, From Heroics to Trust. The days began with communal silent morning prayer, included afternoon Eucharist and closed with communal evening prayer in chapel. Midweek there was a "hermit day" with box lunches and a free afternoon for silence and solitude.

Though silence was strongly encouraged during the nonscheduled moments of the day, the atmosphere was generally more one of sharing ideas than of silence and solitude. Because of the openness of the speakers, their fame and high profile, there was a high energy level among the participants, all of which created an atmosphere in which real silence was quite difficult.

Sister Constance FitzGerald noted that though the vision of the Carmelite Forum had not changed, due to experience "we've learned how to do better what we're doing. We want to enable people to read the Carmelite classics (John of the Cross, Teresa of Avila, Therese of Lisieux and others), and to bring their own lives to interface with these classics." She is amazed how many people return year after year. "It transcends the idea of a seminar. People feel this is a place of prayer and contemplation. They really work with the material, reading and studying the texts." She notes that the reading sessions, in particular, help people to learn and to apply tools for interpretations of the classics.

She commented also that the people react positively and in an interesting way to the two women Carmelites on the Forum: to her and to Sister Vilma Seelaus. "Coming from contemplative life and its experience, we bring something different from what the men bring; we speak closer to our own experience. We have come out of the framework of monastic life and not out of academic education in the same way as the men."

While the seminar could be held in other locations, the advantages of an attractive campus with dormitory housing, ready-made and handy facilities for lectures, various rooms for reading sessions and workshops, all lend themselves, in the eyes of the Carmelite Forum, to continuing the relationship with the Center for Spirituality at St. Mary's.

There was a high level of interest, of sharing, of questioning among the participants. It is an intense and scholarly and, for the most part, "left brain" approach to Carmelite spirituality, though the reading sessions created a balance somewhat. Some members of the Forum felt that without the interpretive expertise of the presenters, lay people would not have sufficient background to plumb the depths of the spiritual classics. Whether that be the case or not, this program obviously fills a need on the part of many people.

FEATURES FOR DISCERNMENT

- Scholarly look at Carmelite Spirituality
- Unparalleled access to renowned Carmelite teachers
- Strong sense of bonding and community among participants
- Uniquely shared reading sessions of the Carmelite classics

SAMPLE SCHEDULE *Therese: Her Mission Today 1897-1997*

Monday, June 24, 1997

8:30-9:00	Morning Prayer
9:15-10:15	"Therese: Child, Girl, Woman"
	Vilma Seelaus, O.C.D.
10:45-11:45	Reading Sessions:
	Chapter One: Childhood Memories
	Chapter Four: First Communion
1:00-2:00	Solitude, Prayer, Study, Leisure
2:00-3:00	Workshops:
	"Spiritual Guidance"
	Kevin Culligan, O.C.D.
	"God in the Human Story"
	Vilma Seelaus, O.C.D.
3:10-4:10	Workshops:
	"Experience of Darkness"
	Constance FitzGerald, O.C.D.
	"Program of Life"
	Ernest Larkin, O.Carm.
	"From Heroics to Trust"
	John Welch, O.Carm.
4:30-5:30	Roman Catholic Eucharist
9:00-9:20	Evening Prayer

■ HESED COMMUNITY

Address: 3745 Elston Ave.
Oakland, California 94602

Phone: 510-482-5573

Type of Contemplative Formation Model: Retreats, workshops, weekly schedule for group meditation, local support groups

Founder: Sister Barbara Hazzard

Director: Sister Barbara Hazzard

Tradition: Christian, Benedictine

Sources: Benedictine Rule, John Main, Scripture

Start-up Date: June 1981

Participant Profile: Participants are drawn from various Christian denominations; approximately eighty-five percent are women, fifteen percent are men. Members of the Hesed Community range in age from the late twenties to the late eighties. Married, single and divorced people are included within the Community's ranks. Members come to Hesed seeking to develop a closer experience with God and to become more peaceful. Some like the balance emphasized in the Rule of St. Benedict. Several hundred people have participated in Hesed Community since its founding.

Newsletter: A newsletter is published four times a year with a circulation of around two hundred and fifty worldwide.

Programs: In addition to its schedule of weekly meditations, *lectio divina* and eucharistic liturgies, Hesed offers occasional workshops on various topics, such as the Enneagram.

Cost: No cost other than donations to support Hesed's work

Hesed (a Hebrew word meaning "God's faithful love") is based in a home in a residential area of Oakland, California. The mission of this Benedictine Community, located in an urban environment, is the teaching and practice of Christian meditation. It was founded in 1984 by Sister Barbara Hazzard. Hesed Community is associated with the World Community for Christian Meditation (the John Main prayer) yet it is incorporated as an autonomous lay contemplative community with a nucleus of approximately fifty members and an additional one hundred members spread throughout the broader community and world.

Maintaining its original vision of 1981, Hesed keeps a simple focus: the practice and teaching of Christian Meditation. Hesed follows and teaches the John Main method of meditation, due, in large part, to Sister Barbara Hazzard's exposure to that method when visiting Dom John Main's Benedictine Priory in Montreal, Canada. The Community's prayer schedule consists of eucharistic liturgies twice a week, *lectio divina* once a week and morning prayer three times a week. All include silent meditation. There are suppers after liturgy once a month, gatherings of the membership twice a year and an annual retreat weekend.

As one of the members stated, "Many seekers don't know where to go to get direction for their spiritual seeking, for guidance and support. We provide it with community, with a lending library of books and tapes. Without places like this, where would the average person go to get help in order to grow spiritually?" Another member stated it this way. "We provide something that is not contradictory but complementary to what other forms of religious structures provide; a deepening to schools of theology, retreats, parishes."

There are different ways of belonging to the Hesed Community. Some come occasionally. Those designated as "family brothers and sisters" attend more regularly, have a higher level of interest, meditate regularly and support the Community in a variety of ways. Lastly, there are the (Benedictine) Oblates who make public promises, support the Community financially, meditate daily and are committed to growing in Benedictine spirituality.

All members agree that the primary benefit to those who come to the Hesed Community is in being with other Christians meditating in a group, the support of the group meditation experience. Being exposed to new ideas and new books also benefits members. "People experience a loss of depth in contemporary life. We help get back in touch with those lost depths," says Sister Barbara. "The presence of the group, the community helps to validate the spiritual journey. There is no cultural validation for this kind of inner journey." Sister Barbara is an experienced spiritual director who offers direction to members upon request.

While Hesed Community is open to persons in all stages of contemplative life and development, it may be particularly helpful to those at the beginning stage of this journey. It offers introductory meditative experiences for beginners and additional support for the beginner's journey through a fairly extensive library of books and videos and audiotapes.

Sister Barbara's dream has long been to have other houses like Hesed, choosing urban places for the layperson who has to be in the urban environment. This is based upon John Main's vision of contemplative community as an integral part of urban life. An urban setting may not offer the natural beauty of some other sites, but it gives the busy layperson a touch of inner solitude and prayer on a daily or frequent basis, a gift that fits more into the needs of today's busy culture.

Hesed's physical environment is a simple home situated in an ordinary neighborhood in Oakland. The lower level of the house has been converted into a small meditation chapel and a larger community chapel along with a lending library. Sister Barbara's dream to have other houses such as the one in the Oakland neighborhood is being realized with another Hesed in San Francisco and one in Auckland, New Zealand.

FEATURES FOR DISCERNMENT

- Autonomous lay contemplative community in urban setting
- Focuses on practice and teaching of Christian meditation
- Supportive community helping to validate and deepen the spiritual journey of the average person
- Various levels of commitment open to the seeker: occasional, "family brothers and sisters" and Oblates
- Ongoing support in community prayer
- Open to all stages of contemplative practice but particularly helpful to beginners

■ PENDLE HILL

Address: 338 Plush Mill Road
Wallingford, Pennsylvania 19086-6099

Phone: 610-566-4507, ext. 142

Fax: 610-566-3679

Type of Contemplative Formation Model: Retreats, courses, workshops, long-term residential opportunities

Founders: A group of the Religious Society of Friends

Director/Dean: Margaret Fraser

Tradition: Religious Society of Friends

Sources: Grounded in the beliefs, traditions and testimonies of the Religious Society of Friends; open to other traditions

Start-up Date: 1930

Participant Profile: Although the majority of participants are from the Religious Society of Friends, there are significant numbers of other seekers as well: priests, ministers, laity of many faiths and some with no formal religious affiliation. Generally there are more women than men in the programs. Usually the participants are middle-aged or older but attempts are being made to highlight programs that will attract younger people as well. Because of financial and other obligations, the majority of participants in most of the programs are single or come by themselves. However, families are welcome in all of the programs and there are several staff families as part of the Pendle Hill community. People come to Pendle Hill because of a desire for spiritual growth, for spiritual refreshment and renewal, to discern their future course, to learn more about the Society of Friends and to discuss Friends issues. Some come to have time to themselves, others to participate in the community life.

Newsletter: Pendle Hill publishes bulletins and brochures announcing their upcoming programs and activities.

Programs: Pendle Hill has a variety of offerings ranging from public lectures to long-term residential programs. Program offerings are in the fields of Quaker history and practice, religious studies, the arts and social and political issues.

Cost (as of June 1999): Each student term costs $4,400. Three terms cost $12,800. Sojourner rates are $62.50 per day, room and board. Conference prices vary but are based on sojourner rates.

West of Philadelphia, on twenty-three acres of wooded and well-landscaped grounds, lies a Quaker center for contemplation and study, Pendle Hill. Founded in 1929, it is named for the hill in England where George Fox, the founder of the Religious Society of Friends, had his vision of a place where all people meet, a place of dialogue where diversity is welcomed and shared with each other.

Pendle Hill has been, for the most part, an expression of "unprogrammed" Eastern Quakerism, meaning there is considerably less emphasis on external expressions of faith such as liturgy, ministers and symbols. It is almost Zen-like in its theological simplicity. Dean Margaret Fraser's response to the inquiry, "What does contemplation mean to you?" exemplifies this simplicity as lived at Pendle Hill. Margaret states, "We don't use the term a lot because one starts to define it...but....a deep relationship with God; so deep it is like breathing air—one doesn't know one does it."

One guest explained this philosophy in an even more practical way. She said "there is varied terminology here (some I'm not used to), but it is incumbent on the listener to pick up meanings, not incumbent upon the speaker to explain.... We're not always turning things into an intellectual debate. People listen and ask questions in order to help the subject discern, not to give advice."

Most people coming to Pendle Hill are drawn through their exposure to Pendle Hill publications: six pamphlets and two books published yearly. People read and want to come to apply that spirituality. Thousands have come in that way. Hundreds come each year for weekend extension programs, and sixty to seventy come yearly for a personal retreat of a day, a week, or two to three weeks. These people are called sojourners.

One of the largest and most organized programs is the resident program, which consists of one eleven-week and two ten-week terms per year. About seventy people participate in this program, half as staff living and working at Pendle Hill and half who come as students. The staff is composed of persons from diverse Christian backgrounds. Courses are offered in biblical studies, Quaker studies, literature and the arts (clay, paper and book-making, music), spiritual practice, social and global concerns, spirituality, ecology, earth ethics, contemplative living, among others.

Woven throughout the curriculum is physical work. Everyone has a daily job in connection with meals and a weekly job caring for a public living space. In addition one morning a week all work together (some in silence) at some physical manual labor. There seems to be a lightness of spirit about the work which gives balance between head and hands. Work is seen as a spiritual discipline. There are talks about the spirituality of work.

Every morning all are invited to gather for one half-hour of silent worship. In the manner of the Quaker tradition, the silence of listening may become an opportunity for someone to speak as the Spirit moves the community gathered together. There is also silence at various times of the day: before meals, in classes, in late evening prayer and every Wednesday afternoon, which is reserved for those practicing silent contemplation.

There is a cultural richness here, for people come from all over the world. And there is laughter and some boisterous community, for children often live here with their parents who are on staff.

Pendle Hill is located on a twenty-three-acre campus, with thirteen buildings for residents and sojourners, a main house where meals are taken together and a "barn" with a grange or meeting room for worship. There are two hermitages available, one for day visits only and an overnight hermitage surrounded by a bamboo grove.

Each student in the resident program has a consultant for a weekly conversation. The student may choose any staff member—a maintenance person, for example—as his or her consultant. The structure and life-style are egalitarian throughout, rather than hierarchical.

Though around sixty percent of those who come to Pendle Hill are Quakers, Dean Margaret Fraser's vision for the future encourages all to come. "I want us to be a place that welcomes people in all stages of doubt and faith, and all religious backgrounds, to be equipped to leave this place and go and serve the world in whatever way they need. I want it to be a place of transformation."

FEATURES FOR DISCERNMENT

- Society of Friends (Quaker) heritage emphasizing egalitarianism and spirituality of work
- Focus primarily educational
- Little emphasis on external symbols or expressions of faith

■ RESOURCES FOR ECUMENICAL SPIRITUALITY

Address: 3704 Highway 13
Dunnegan, Missouri 65640-9705
(Forest Monastery)

Phone: 417-754-2562

Type of Contemplative Formation Model: Retreats, workshops, courses, long-term residential opportunities

Founder: Mary Jo Meadow

Director: Mary Jo Meadow

Tradition: Christian, Roman Catholic, Theravadan Buddhism

Sources: Carmelite mystics especially John of the Cross, vipassana meditation

Start-up Date: 1987

Participant Profile: Anyone is welcome. Retreats usually have about thirty-five to forty percent women religious. Some priests usually attend. Also attending regularly are Protestant clergy from various denominations, predominantly Episcopalian. Laywomen and men make up the balance. The ratio of women to men is usually two to one. The same mix come to the Forest Monastery for practice. Participants tend to be middle-aged or older, with the majority in their forties or fifties; few are under thirty. Some participants are married, but most are not. There are about seventy-five new retreatants per year. The Forest Monastery, started in late 1993, has between twelve to fifteen visitors a year who stay for a prolonged period.

Newsletter: *The RES Newsletter* for members is published three times a year. A mailing list of 3,100 receives information each fall about RES programs for the coming year and also information on becoming a member. This mailing explains vipassana meditation and insight meditation retreats as well as giving the retreat schedule for the upcoming year with a profile of the retreat leaders.

Programs: Silence and awareness retreats, based on the teachings of Saint John of the Cross and vipassana (insight) meditation practice, come from the Christian Carmelite and Theravadan Buddhist traditions. Each day offers an integrative conference, meditation instructions, group meditation sittings and walking practice. RES (Resources for Ecumenical Spirituality) also offers insight meditation retreats for Twelve Step programs, a general Buddhist-Christian retreat, retreats with various other themes, and some simple insight meditation retreats without a theme. The loving kindness retreat teaches a Buddhist method for developing loving and compassionate attitudes toward all beings. Insight meditation retreats emphasize interior and exterior silence, awareness of all experiences, and alternating sitting and walking meditation. RES programs are offered at various locations around the United States and in Australia.

Cost: Varies with retreats and locations. Fees do not include honoraria for the teachers. In keeping with a 2,500-year-old Buddhist tradition of putting no cost on the teachings, the teachers ask for nothing but their expenses (however, freewill offerings are accepted).

RES is a nonprofit corporation established to foster mutual understanding among religious faiths through shared spiritual practice and dialogue. RES sponsors retreats, colloquia, workshops, publications and other projects related to spiritual practice and study.

RES was founded in 1987 by Mary Jo Meadow, emerita professor of psychology and director of the religious studies program at Mankato State University in Mankato, Minnesota. Mary Jo has a Ph.D. in psychology, specializing in clinical and personality, and a subspecialty in the psychology of religions. While in her twenties, Mary Jo had a spiritual director whose love of John of the Cross led her to read him; thus her whole spiritual life unfolded around John of the Cross. When the last of her eight children left home, Mary Jo took a sabbatical year and explored programs of spiritual practice throughout the United States. She had been only a few days at a three-month vipassana retreat at the Insight Meditation Society in Barre, Massachusetts, when she said to herself, "This is John of the Cross!

135

This is how to do what John of the Cross says we have to do!" Out of those insights she approached Father Kevin Culligan, a famous Carmelite scholar and a friend. She and Father Kevin were both members of the American Psychological Association (APA). Together they presented a paper to the APA entitled, "Similarities between Carmelite Spirituality and Buddhist Meditation: A Psychological Analysis." After additional presentations on the theory, they decided to offer a Christian retreat using insight meditation practice as a method to lead the practitioner "toward the emptiness in sense and spirit that John of the Cross maintains is a necessary disposition for union with God." Mary Jo quotes John of the Cross in saying, "God does not fit in an occupied heart." Since insight meditation is a technique, it in itself does not demand belief in the tenets of Buddhist religion.

Thus, in 1987, they began the series of eight-day retreats called "silence and awareness retreats" led by Mary Jo, Kevin Culligan, O.C.D., and Daniel Chowning, O.C.D. From 1989 to 1993, one hundred and seventy persons made the retreat, some more than once. As the numbers grew, the team began in 1994 to offer additional silence and awareness retreats in different parts of the country.

Silence is maintained throughout the retreat and meals are simple, usually vegetarian. Daily Eucharist is celebrated, the Sacrament of Reconciliation is offered and daily conferences explain the relationship of insight meditation practice to the deepening of Christian faith, hope and love. "Within this Christian context the entire insight meditation practice, both sitting and walking, is taught in a classical manner in all its integrity so that retreatants can learn it fully within eight days," states Mary Jo.

The retreat itself in twelve cassettes is available through Credence Cassettes, as are several books by the three leaders of the silence and awareness retreats. Kevin Culligan has named the practice Christian insight meditation to emphasize its Christian theology and to differentiate the practice from John Main's Christian Meditation or Thomas Keating's Centering Prayer.

As part of RES, "stillness and knowing retreats" are offered which are geared less to the spirituality of John of the Cross and are more general Christian-Buddhist retreats.

More recently, the "serenity and insight retreat," based on the Twelve Steps program, has been offered.

The teachers are not paid for their retreats other than expenses and the opportunity for a freewill offering on the part of retreatants.

The retreats use established retreat facilities across the country so the retreat is priced at cost—for use of facility and room and board. Mary Jo emphasizes that "RES will never sell spiritual teachers. Guests are given opportunity to give in return."

In 1993 RES purchased the Forest Monastery, forty-five minutes north of Springfield, Missouri, in a northern finger of the Ozarks. An air-conditioned, five-bedroom house sits on thirty-five heavily wooded acres; five bedrooms are available for private retreatants. There is also a primitive A-frame cabin. In 1997 Mary Jo retired from Mankato State University and moved to the Forest Monastery permanently. Retreats will continue there on a structured and individual basis.

RES members (one hundred and fifty) pay yearly dues of $20. They receive three newsletters a year, priority registration on retreats, and tapes and books at the RES authors' price. The mailing list for the RES newsletter is thirty-one hundred which includes members, non-members and friends. Two-thirds to three-fourths of the RES members have an ongoing relationship with RES, making yearly retreats.

Mary Jo, a secular Carmelite and a member of Sisters for Christian Community, has been given the precepts of Theravadan nuns by the monastic head of this lineage, the venerable Sayadau U. Pandita of Burma. She feels the external environment for RES retreats is unimportant for "this is an interior journey." She points out that RES is not working with institutions but with individuals, helping to teach a practice whereby individual people can come to have "that openness and purity" that allows for John of the Cross' definition of contemplation: "the inflow of God into the substance of the soul."

The qualifications of the teachers are impressive, coming out of a background of scholarship and practice of Carmelite spirituality. Their work follows in the footsteps of Saint Thomas Aquinas who adapted much of Aristotle to Christian teaching. It also follows the guidelines of Vatican II which "exhorts Catholic Christians to 'acknowledge, preserve and promote the spiritual and moral goods and cultural values of Hinduism and Buddhism.'"

Purifying the Heart: Buddhist Insight Meditations for Christians, by Kevin Culligan, Mary Jo Meadow and Daniel Chowning, both explains the relationship of Christian contemplation with insight meditation and offers readers an understanding of the practice in the context of the Christian life. It is an excellent beginning for the spiritual seeker who wishes to learn more about contemplation, how to empty oneself and find God. Since the retreats are quite intense, they offer the more advanced seeker deeper opportunities for spiritual growth and inner discipline in contemplative and meditative practice.

FEATURES FOR DISCERNMENT

- Extremely structured programs with high level of commitment necessary
- Basically Christian teaching but draws upon Buddhist vipassana meditation practice
- Prolonged periods of meditation sitting and silence
- Uses established retreat facilities across the United States
- Simple vegetarian meals

SAMPLE RETREAT SCHEDULE

6:30	Rising
7:00	Roman Catholic Eucharist
7:45	Breakfast
8:45	Sitting Meditation and Instruction
10:00	Walking Meditation
11:00	Sitting Meditation
11:45	Walking Meditation or
	Integration Questions and Answers
12:30	Lunch
	Optional Walking Meditation
2:15	Sitting Meditation
3:00	Walking Meditaton
3:45	Sitting Meditation and Instruction
4:45	Walking Meditation
5:15	Loving-Kindness Practice
6:00	Supper
	Optional Walking Meditation
7:30	Retreat Conference
8:30	Walking Meditation
9:15	Sitting Meditation
10:00	Further Practice or Rest

■ ASSOCIATION OF CONTEMPLATIVE SISTERS

Address: ACS Central Office:

Carmelite Monastery
2500 Cold Spring Road
Indianapolis, Indiana 46222

Office of the President (1998-2000)
710-264 Queens Quay West
Toronto, Ontario, Canada M5J 1B5

Phone: 416-260-0575

Fax: 416-260-3404

Type of Contemplative Formation Model: International network, local support groups

Founders: Core group of members from contemplative communities

President: Sister Rosalie Bertell, G.N.S.H.

Tradition: Christian, Roman Catholic

Sources: Primarily contemplative prayer traditions of Western Church, open to prayer practices of the East

Start-up Date: 1969

Participant Profile: An estimated thirty-five percent are members of Catholic contemplative orders, fifteen percent are members of Catholic apostolic religious communities, forty-six percent are lay Catholic women and the remaining four percent are women from other religious denominations or those who have no affiliation to a particular Church. Their primary reason for joining ACS is to experience nourishment and support on the contemplative path. At the present time ACS is primarily a women's organization, although men are welcomed as friends of the Association (as distinct from members and along with women who support the Association's goals but do not wish to actively participate as members). Status as an ACS friend enables one to attend some meetings as well as to receive the national newsletter.

Newsletter: *ACS National Newsletter* published quarterly with a circulation of approximately five hundred members and friends. ACS regional newsletters published quarterly and distributed by each region within its locale.

Programs: A biennial general assembly carried out successively in each of the five regions with presenters addressing topics relevant to contemplative living organized around a central theme; regional meetings in alternate years with resource persons addressing topics relevant to contemplative living, organized around a particular theme. Members have opportunities for prayer and sharing at both events.

Cost: Annual membership $35; Friends contribution $15.

The Association of Contemplative Sisters is a network of five hundred women whose purpose is to foster, nourish and support the contemplative journey of its members. Past President Ginny Manss explained, "Its primary purpose has been to be an *association*. Its business is *isness*. One of its original goals, the one that has endured through the years, is to nourish the contemplative dimension of women (primarily) and men."

The ACS was organized in 1969, at that time drawing members from at least thirty-five different orders of canonical contemplative religious women. Following Vatican II, these women felt a need for mutual support and a renewed understanding of contemplative religious life. The sisters spoke of a "desire within humankind for a deeper human life and an authentic response to the Father in Christ." The ACS at that time committed itself to the "development of a greater appreciation and clearer expression of our role as reflectors of this desire in society." Thomas Merton was among those giving guidance in the formative years prior to formal organization.

Through the years, more women were drawn to the Association. In 1986 laywomen were accepted into full membership. Today, ACS is "unique among contemplative organizations and associations in that its membership is composed of a blend of lay and religious, those in canonical contemplative communities and those who are not." This rich blend includes sisters in monastic and other religious communities, married and widowed women, single laywomen, consecrated virgins, hermits and women in lay contemplative communities. This blending and compatibility was further enriched when, in 1992, the first laywoman was elected as national president of ACS.

There is a spiritual range and diversity among the members of ACS. Some are newly acquainted with the contemplative dimension of life and are seeking ever greater depth and understanding. Other members have spent the major portion of their lives on the contemplative path and, subsequently, are enriching others through their own example and through their writings and teaching. The variety of ministries among the members is as numerous as the members themselves. Many have advanced degrees and serve as pastoral ministers, counselors, authors, spiritual directors. And many hold simple and unassuming jobs offering service in the marketplace or in the home.

All are united in one unique way. Each one seems to place above all a priority to live out with all of the depth of one's being a full response to one's contemplative call, a willingness (or demand) to see and respond to life with "different eyes." The members see life not in terms of goals to be achieved but in terms of openness to be shaped by "a reality beyond our own" to quote Wendy Wright, a member from Creighton University.

This focus, however it may be expressed or manifested outwardly in members' lives, creates a tangible example and support for new members. "Because," as Ginny Manss said, "it has always officially kept itself free from backing or putting its energies into specific causes, it's free to go where the Spirit leads."

As a result of its one focus, "ACS has always been prophetic in nature. Its origins benefited the institutional Church, but it has grown beyond that, a parallel growth," says former President Manss. It has always expressed openness to other religions and welcomes the sound and proven riches of other contemplative traditions. It is open to exposure and depth from our own varied Western contemplative traditions and techniques of prayer but also those from the East as well. "ACS is distinctive," Manss reflects, "in that it has a foot in the lay world as well as the monastic world. It is a reality where those two worlds can come together and be as one. That also is its prophetic stance."

The Association is divided into five geographic regions across the United States and Canada, and further subdivided into local clusters. There is a national ACS newsletter published quarterly as well as quarterly regional newsletters. In addition there are regional telephone chains to keep members informed of current news and information. Through local cluster meetings held "as the Spirit moves" within each region, members try to keep in touch with one another often enough to be one family in support and encouragement on this sometimes lonely and primarily hidden dimension and path through life in the world today.

Members pay $35 annual dues to help cover the cost of operation. Prospective members are asked to share briefly, in writing, how they presently respond to their contemplative call within the context of their life-style, why they wish to join, what they hope to receive and contribute as a member, and how they found out about ACS.

ACS seems well placed at this moment in history. It is open to the Spirit as the world changes, yet consciously retains its contemplative stance and depth in a culture trying to accomplish everything, even union with God, "better and faster." It offers a sound, hopeful, model for the future. ACS provides a forum for sharing one's vision and envisioning a shared future; perhaps that's one of its greatest assets. From its very beginning down to the present, contemplative women gather together to dream and to dare to change.

FEATURES FOR DISCERNMENT

- Focuses on deepening one's own contemplative practice and provides an environment for sharing one's contemplative vision
- Distinctive in spiritual depth, breadth and rich life experience of its diverse membership
- Open to different levels of participation as member or friend
- In some regions, local support groups sharing prayer and vision

■ WORLD COMMUNITY FOR CHRISTIAN MEDITATION CHRISTIAN MEDITATION CENTER AND JOHN MAIN INSTITUTE

Address: 3727 Abbeywood
Pearland, Texas, 77584

Phone/Fax: 281-412-9803

London WCCM Fax: 011-44-171-937-6790

Type of Contemplative Formation Model: International network; retreats, courses, workshops; local support groups

Founder: John Main, O.S.B.

National Coordinator: Carla Cooper

Tradition: Christian, Roman Catholic

Sources: Cassian, early Desert Fathers; Jesus Prayer; *The Cloud of Unknowing*; teachings of John Main, Laurence Freeman, Abhishiktananda, William Johnston, Bede Griffiths

Start-up Dates: 1975, first Christian Meditation Center opened in London, England, by John Main, O.S.B.; 1991, World Community of Christian Meditation formally organized.

Participant Profile: Thirteen hundred members active in meditation groups in the United States. There are more women than men in the groups with ages ranging from thirty-five to eighty. There are more Roman Catholics than other denominations and some with no religious affiliation. Members come from all states of life: religious, single, married, divorced.

Newsletters: *U.S. Christian Meditation* quarterly newsletter with a circulation of about four thousand in the United States; quarterly international newsletter circulated throughout thirty-five countries around the world. Coeditors in the United States: Rev. Peter DeMarco and Patt Gulick, 193 Wilton Road West, Ridgefield, Connecticut 06877.

Internet: For information on access to e-mail list for discussion of Christian Meditation, the works of John Main and Laurence Freeman and the work of the WCCM, contact Greg Ryan: *gjryan@aol.com*.

Programs: A variety of programs are offered. An annual John Main Seminar alternates between Europe, North America and the Philippines. Information on current seminars, retreats, and so on can be obtained from the Christian Meditation Center.

Cost: Varies with each offering.

In 1975 a Benedictine monk, Father John Main, opened the first Christian Meditation Center in London, England. In 1977 he came to Montreal, Canada, becoming prior of the Benedictine Monastery. He began to teach a way of prayer—contemplative, non-discursive meditation—to lay men and women interested in deepening their prayer life. He called his method of prayer "Christian Meditation," though it is often spoken of as the "John Main" type of prayer. His instructions were simple. "Sit quietly each morning and evening for twenty to thirty minutes. Silently, interiorly begin to say a single word—*maranatha* (an Aramaic word meaning 'Come, Lord')." This simple (but not easy) form of mantra prayer was taught by the fifth-century Christian monk, Cassian, by the early desert fathers and by the medieval author of *The Cloud of Unknowing*. This contemplative practice of meditation has a rich tradition in the Christian Church; it is an authentic part of the teaching on prayer. Father Main brought this meditation to life again by teaching ever larger groups of people to meditate. Meditation groups sprang up in Canada (there are approximately five hundred members in the greater Toronto area alone and four hundred meditation groups across Canada), throughout the United States, and presently in thirty-five countries throughout the world.

John Main died in 1982. His successor, Father Laurence Freeman, O.S.B., has carried on the work of teaching this contemplative prayer and is the director of the World Community for Christian Meditation.

In 1991 the World Community for Christian Meditation was formally organized to coordinate the work of advancing and sharing the teachings of John Main throughout the world. Also in 1991, the John Main Institute was formed, a legal entity, to fund annual John Main seminars and newsletters.

A John Main seminar is sponsored each year, presenting internationally known authors, speakers and contemplative practitioners, outstanding spiritual leaders of the contemplative life in the world. There have been thirteen annual seminars to date with such outstanding speakers as Father Bede Griffiths, O.S.B., His Holiness the Dalai Lama of Tibet, Father William Johnston, S.J., Raimon Panikkar and Father Laurence Freeman, O.S.B. The 1996 seminar had two hundred and fifty participants from around the world.

Christian Meditation Centers throughout the world and in the United States coordinate the hundreds of Christian Meditation groups and serve as a resource for books and tapes by John Main and Laurence Freeman, the speakers at the annual seminars and other authors on contemplative prayer.

A quarterly international newsletter shares news and notices of retreats across the world. The international newsletter always includes a multipage letter from Father Freeman sharing in depth on contemplative prayer, its place in one's life, along with deeper understandings of what goes on interiorly in one who practices daily meditation. It is a thought-provoking and meaty contemplative treatise each quarter.

This program teaches, practices and educates lay Christians in the way of contemplative prayer without added-on monastic forms or rituals. Its many resources are brought to bear to help a seeker find, and continue in, a way of contemplative formation suitable in the marketplace. Medio Media, Inc., is a good resource for both media materials and for prayer. The worldwide growth of this type of prayer, the quality of speakers willing to participate in the John Main seminars and the soundness of the type of prayer with its historical ties and solid roots in the Church all lead to the not-surprising growth and development of the Christian Meditation movement within the world community.

At present in the United States, there are about thirteen hundred members active in meditation groups. In 1996 plans were under way in the United States to coordinate a school for teachers of this tradition to help facilitate this teaching by offering more formal training.

FEATURES FOR DISCERNMENT

- International grass roots network
- Annual international seminars with renowned spiritual leaders
- Readily accessible practice for lay contemplatives in everyday life
- Simple and consistent instruction on contemplative prayer
- Outstanding spiritual treatises in newsletter

■ SHANTIVANAM

Address: 22019 Meagher Road
Easton, Kansas 66020-7038

Phone: 913-773-8255

Fax: 913-773-5708

Type of Contemplative Formation Model: Long-term residential opportunities, hermitage, house of prayer

Founder: Rev. Edward Hays

Director: Jennifer Sullivan

Tradition: Christian, Roman Catholic

Sources: Blending of East-West traditions

Start-up Date: 1972

Participant Profile: Men and women from a wide range of religious denominations visit Shantivanam, though the majority are Roman Catholic or other Christians; sixty-five percent of participants are women and thirty-five percent are men. There are some married couples, some religious and many single people ranging in age from eighteen upward. People come to Shantivanam for solitude, prayer and the opportunity to pray with a contemplative lay community. Their average length of stay is four days. An average of fifteen hundred to two thousand guests visit Shantivanam each year.

Newsletter: *The Forest Letter* is a bimonthly newsletter of spiritual support with a circulation of about four thousand.

Programs: Shantivanam exists primarily to be a house of prayer for all peoples. There are opportunities for solitude and prayer lasting from one-day visits to one-year sabbaticals. Spiritual companionship with a staff member is available upon request. Shantivanam has offered directed retreats since the fall of 1997. Days of prayer for groups are offered three to four times a year.

Cost: Varies with number of days and types of accommodations. Request current brochure for specific cost list.

Shantivanam, whose name means "Forest of Peace" in Sanskrit, is nestled into one hundred and twenty acres of forest and Kansas prairie land northwest of Kansas City. Envisioned and proposed by former Archbishop Ignatius J. Strecker of Kansas City, Shantivanam was founded by Rev. Edward Hays in 1972. Father Hays, a diocesan priest, was asked to open a house of prayer for both religious and laity living in community and to become its first director. Prior to opening Shantivanam, Father Hays went on a global pilgrimage of shrines and worship centers of the world's prominent religions, which would later leave its influence on the house of prayer as well as the many books he would author. The land chosen as the proposed site for Shantivanam initially had only a tin-roofed horse barn, which would serve as the main building. Within six months after its opening a small group of lay people had joined the house of prayer. A chapel was added to the horse barn and, gradually, hermitages were built for guests and staff. Today there are five simple, primitive cabins (no plumbing) scattered throughout the heavily wooded forest about ten to fifteen minutes' walking distance from the main building that houses the chapel and dining room. There are also seven cabins with complete bath facilities for long-term solitude sabbatical experiences. In addition, there are three rooms in a guest wing of the main building. Currently there are five staff members. The majority of the staff has always been laity.

Shantivanam is primarily a house of prayer so it does not offer retreats or counseling. Those guests who come—and there have been many—do so to "step into an existing prayer life, an ongoing prayer life of this lay community," says Father Ed Hays. The second director in Shantivanam's twenty-four-year history, Father Joe Nassal, was chosen by Father Hays to succeed him in 1995. Father Joe also stressed that "our primary apostolate is prayer, our ministry is prayer." This is a lay community whose "work" is prayer. Those guests who are drawn to this lovely and peace-filled spot are an over-flow or fruit of Shantivanam.

The physical environment is consciously and deliberately chosen and planned with a spirit of simplicity, a lack of clutter and artificial-ity. As nearly as possible the natural surroundings outside are incor-porated inside. The chapel is walled with large glass windows that look onto redbud trees, ponds and forest. There is no need for stained glass in such a place.

The kitchen, dining room and library still retain the rough wood-en walls of the original horse barn. Guests eat with staff at the long wooden refectory table, sharing simple but plentiful food and con-versation. Rock gardens, wooden bridges and paths surround the main building. The architecture and attention to detail warm the soul with beauty.

Three times daily a bell is rung (fifteen minutes ahead) and all go to chapel for one half-hour of prayer: 7:00 a.m., noon and 5:00 p.m. The bell can be heard in the woods, calling those in the hermitages.

There is a weekly rhythm at Shantivanam. Thursday is a solitude day for staff and guests. The other days of the week are communal days with optional participation in prayers and meals. Guests enter into that established rhythm, the dance between solitude and commu-nity. As Father Joe says, "There is a holy order here that is not oppres-sive...one drinks from a deeper well."

FEATURES FOR DISCERNMENT

- Beautifully rustic, simple accommodations that integrate the nat-ural surroundings
- An archdiocesan lay community whose work is prayer
- Balanced rhythm between community and solitude
- Unstructured except for three periods of community prayer
- Enticing sense of peace and tranquillity

SAMPLE SCHEDULE

On a Communal Day

7:00	Liturgy (Friday) Morning Prayer (Saturday)
7:30	Pick-up Breakfast
11:45	Noon Prayer
12:00	Noontime Meal
5:00	Evening Prayer
5:30	Evening Meal

Sunday

7:30	Pick-up Breakfast
8:40	Pre-liturgy Meditation
9:00	Liturgy of the Eucharist
10:15	Reception for Liturgy Visitors *(optional for weekend guests)*
11:30	Brunch
12:00-2:30	Departure Time

■ NADA HERMITAGE—SPIRITUAL LIFE INSTITUTE

Address: #1 Carmelite Way
Crestone, Colorado 81131

Phone: 719-256-1778

Fax: 719-256-4719

Type of Contemplative Formation Model: Retreats, courses, workshops, monastic community with structured live-in, community with formal and informal support network, hermitage

Founder: William McNamara, O.C.D.

Directors: William McNamara, O.C.D., and Mother Tessa Bielecki

Prior: Father David Denny

Tradition: Christian, Roman Catholic, Carmelite Sources: Teresa of Avila, John of the Cross

Start-up Date: Program—1960; Site—1983

Participant Profile: Mainly Roman Catholic but a number from other Christian and non-Christian denominations. Approximately fifty percent women, fifty percent men. Since 1986 there have been over fifteen hundred individuals of all ages, married, single and religious, who have participated in the programs. Participants come to seek God through an experience of solitude and desert wilderness.

Newsletter: *Forefront* is a quarterly magazine that includes essays, poetry and art, evoking a spirit of contemplation.

Programs: Primarily personal, private "hermitage" retreats with some minimal direction available. Participants may join the Nada monks in their times of daily community prayer. Many books and tapes are available in hermitages and main building. Affiliates are "soul-friended" through a specific program utilizing books, tapes and more.

Cost (as of June 1999): Hermitages are $50 for the first day and $40 for each additional day. Couples may share a hermitage for $60 the first day and $50 thereafter. Cost includes board and room.

The Spiritual Life Institute was established by William McNamara, a Discalced Carmelite Father. In 1967 property was purchased in Sedona, Arizona, and the Nada community began with the arrival of Mother Tessa Bielecki who worked closely with Father McNamara. It spread in 1972 to Kemptville, Nova Scotia, where Nova Nada was established. In the early 1980's the community was given seventy acres of valley and thirty acres of mountain in the beautiful Sangre de Cristo Mountain range, which overlooks the desert of San Luis Valley in Crestone, Colorado. The community transferred its site from Sedona to the more secluded Crestone area. In 1993, at the request of an Irish bishop, another site was begun in Ireland. Today there are twenty-one Institute core members spread throughout these three sites.

The Nada community at Crestone speaks of an "earthy mysticism" that takes a long, loving look at life, especially nature. Thus all creatures, as well as the land itself, are perceived as pointing to the "Ultimate Reality" as a "personal presence." In accord with this belief the members use sound ecological practices: composting, passive solar houses that are bermed into the hillside, recycling, eating "natural foods" and more.

While Father McNamara is a Discalced Carmelite, the other men and women take simple vows and are bound by Roman Catholic canon law as hermits. They follow the Carmelite tradition of Teresa of Avila and John of the Cross, and wear simple brown habits for prayer, meeting guests and for shared meals, of which there are two per week following a Mass. Liturgies take place in the beautiful Sangre de Cristo chapel which, along with the main Agape building, appears to grow out of the earth, oriented toward the sun to harness its heat. The architecture of all the buildings is organic, rooted in the earth and combining medieval and contemporary traditional southwestern styles. There are sixteen hermitages, several of which are used by the community members. Usually there is room for six to ten guests.

Nada is a Spanish word meaning "nothing." The Spiritual Life Institute believes that this word reflects the theology of John of the Cross and that those who follow this way are concerned with nothing but God and God's kingdom. Affiliates, those who wish to be more closely connected with the Nada core group because they have been retreatants, *Forefront* readers and friends are called "de Nadans," meaning of the Nada spiritual family. The Nada Institute members are willing to act as "soul-friends" with the Affiliates, trying through their publications and other communication to support ordinary people where they live and work. A de Nadan is encouraged toward daily meditative reading, artistic leisure work such as music, poetry, artwork and writing, simplification of life-style and daily periods of solitude and prayer. Creative involvement by the community in nature, artistic and scholarly pursuits have been essential dimensions of Nada spirituality since the Institute's beginning.

The Nada members lead missions, give lectures and workshops, teach, give retreats and work on their publications. They also participate in the daily round of chores, including working in an organic garden to provide some of their own vegetables for meals. There's a spirit of quiet and solitude during their work which is greatly augmented by the stark, yet beautiful surroundings.

The overall sense is one of deep solitude and great natural beauty enhanced by daily communal lauds and vespers. Guests are invited to participate or not, as they choose. Guests are also asked to join in a shared Saturday work period. One week of every month is set aside for a period of prayer, fasting and total solitude. An ordinary schedule for the community includes lauds and vespers shared daily at 6:00 a.m. and 5:00 p.m., except during Catholic Mass times on Wednesday and Sunday mornings and Friday evenings. Mass on Friday evenings and Sunday mornings is followed by the two shared meals of the week. Saturday evening also includes Benediction followed by Exposition of the Blessed Sacrament. Individuals sign up for an hour of prayer throughout Saturday night. Sunday is a day of leisure when the Nadans "waste the day by praying and playing."

FEATURES FOR DISCERNMENT

- Semi-isolated, rugged, beautiful desert mountain terrain
- Ecological sensitivity in life-style and buildings
- Support for affiliates through "soul-friending," publications, other communication
- Unstructured with high degree of silence and solitude

■ OSAGE MONASTERY

Address: 18701 W. Monastery Road
 Sand Springs, Oklahoma 74063

Phone: 918-245-2734

Type of Contemplative Formation Model: Retreats, monastic community with structured live-ins, long-term residential opportunities, ashram, hermitage

Founder: Sister Pascaline Coff, O.S.B., Benedictine Sisters of Perpetual Adoration, St. Louis

Director: Sister Pascaline Coff, O.S.B.

Tradition: Christian, Roman Catholic, Benedictine, ashram

Sources: Christian Zen, Ruben Habito, Father Bede Griffiths, the desert fathers and mothers, Meister Eckhart, Spiritual Exercises, Centering Prayer, Vipassana, Jesus Prayer, Philokalia, Intermonastic Dialogue

Start-up Date: June 1980

Participant Profile: Men and women of various Judeo-Christian and Eastern backgrounds come to Osage Monastery seeking deeper meaning and a deeper prayer life. Ages range from twenty-eight to seventy-five. Approximately two-thirds of the participants are women, one-third men. Clergy, religious, lay religious, married, single and divorced people are all welcome. Retreatants number two hundred and forty per year plus guests who come for shorter visits.

Programs: Participants experience contemplative prayer in a monastic ashram life-style; adoration as a way of life combines with and complements the pursuit of peace and justice. Average length of retreat is six to eight days. Temporary membership in community for a discerned length of time is an option. Also offered: Christian Zen retreats; live conferences; contemplative outreach videos; two hours' contemplative sitting in common daily, divine office; solitude day weekly; spiritual direction as discerned mutually.

Cost: Freewill offering for guests and retreatants.

Near the Arkansas river, on forty-three acres of forest in Eastern Oklahoma that the Osage Native Americans once called home, stands a Christian monastic ashram. Osage Monastery was founded by Sister Pascaline Coff and the Benedictine Sisters of Perpetual Adoration in 1980 as a contemplative community to give testimony to simplicity and top priority to contemplative prayer and its atmosphere. An ashram is a spiritual center in which there is a teacher or teachers and where people come to share in the good works and deeds of the Lord. An ashram has these qualifying marks: It is open to all religions; it has a simplified life-style; it has intense spiritual exercises.

The main building, in the center of the forest, is the common house containing a unique chapel, a dining room, a community room with fireplace and a library filled with Eastern and Western spiritual classics. On one side of the common house are eight community hermitages scattered in the forest connected by pathways to the common house. On the other side are six guest hermitages. The grounds and connecting pathways (graveled) give a sense of orderliness and tranquillity, a peaceful harmony of man-made structure and nature.

The chapel itself has glassed walls that let in the seasons to speak their own prayer. The center of the hardwood chapel floor is sunken, incorporating the symbol of the American Indian sacred sun dance circle. On the sides of the chapel are areas for private meditation with symbols famous among the religions of both East and West. One can easily sense a deep cosmic unity in this sacred space.

There is a definite monastic rhythm at Osage as well as a deliberate sense of cultural healing and bringing together of East and West in deepest forms of prayer and meditation without diluting the richness and truths of Christianity. On Mondays there is special solitude for community and guests, so there are no common prayers or meals. Tuesdays through Saturdays begin with silent meditation for an hour, followed by morning prayer and communion service. Noon prayer is followed by community dinner. Late afternoon there is another hour of silent meditation (all voluntary) followed by Vespers and supper. Following supper is faith sharing or a presentation or video or slide show, then Compline and silence until the next morning after communion. During the day there is a silent though not austere atmosphere. The attitude among the community and guests is quietness.

Meals are simple, vegetarian, but plentiful, eaten together at a long wooden table with bench seats. The hermitages are simple, rectangular, one-room cabins with a bed (consisting of a mattress on a board frame), a desk and chair, and a small table in one corner with a candle and icon and an arm chair for prayer. Each cabin has its own modern bathroom complete with shower.

There is an opportunity for temporary membership in the community at Osage for six months to a year. Such members visit with the community prior to their coming and enter into discernment with the community after the first three months as a way of evaluating their experience.

Anyone is welcome for a period of retreat at Osage. Though the usual length of retreat is between six to eight days, some retreatants stay for a month or longer. One may make a Christian Zen retreat if desired. Ordinarily participants enter into the rhythm of the monastic schedule and may avail themselves of spiritual direction from well-qualified members of the community. Sister Pascaline Coff, founder and current director of Osage, obtained her Ph.D. in theology from St. Mary's College, Notre Dame. She likewise spent a year at Father Bede Griffiths' ashram in south India (considered one of the best Hindu-Christian centers in that country) prior to founding Osage Monastery.

Father Bede Griffiths visited the forest in which Osage is now located, offering Eucharist and blessing the four directions, calling down God's peace and love on all who were at that moment entering into the ancient and sacred tradition of forest dwellers, as well as all who would visit there. That blessing of peace has extended to the present day where it continues to make itself known in the forest and in the community at Osage.

FEATURES FOR DISCERNMENT

- Christian ashram monastery
- Conscious commitment to embrace and share the riches of other cultures and religions
- For beginners and the more advanced
- Tangible sense of orderliness, simplicity and tranquillity

- Welcoming freedom to participate in silent meditation and monastic rhythm
- Traditional yet innovative Benedictine monastic community

■ LITTLE PORTION HERMITAGE

Address: Rt. 7 Box 608
Eureka Springs, Arkansas 72632

Phone: 501-253-7710

Type of Contemplative Formation Model: Monastic community with structured live-ins

Founder: John Michael Talbot

Director: John Michael Talbot, general minister

Tradition: Christian, Roman Catholic, Franciscan, Benedictine

Sources: Traditions of Eastern and Western monasticism

Start-up Date: 1983

Participant Profile: Current adult members of the Brothers and Sisters of Charity range in age from twenty-three to seventy-six. There are six celibate brothers, six celibate sisters, one single person and three families (six adults and one child). The community has a Roman Catholic base, but an ecumenical orientation.

Newsletter: A newsletter is published twice a year communicating recent events at Little Portion Hermitage as well as John Michael Talbot's concert schedule for upcoming months. John Michael's books and recordings are advertised as well as the retreat and workshop schedule for Little Portion Retreat and Training Center.

Internet: *http://www.john-michaeltalbot.org/jmt.html*

Programs: Little Portion Hermitage offers no formal programs or retreats. A full schedule of retreats is offered at the Little Portion Retreat and Training Center also located in Eureka Springs. Guests are welcome to visit the Hermitage at specified times. People interested in joining the monastic community are introduced into a gradual process of mutual discernment. Full incorporation into the community requires a lengthy period of formation.

Cost: Varies with program at Little Portion Retreat and Training Center

Nestled in a valley surrounded by hills and lush rolling farmland in northeastern Arkansas is Little Portion Hermitage, the home of the Brothers and Sisters of Charity. Founded by John Michael Talbot, nationally known composer, concert artist and spiritual writer, this fully integrated monastic community had its start at Alverna Franciscan Center in Indianapolis, Indiana, in 1979-80. In 1983 the community established its monastic motherhouse, Little Portion Hermitage, in the Ozark mountains near the resort town of Eureka Springs, Arkansas. The Brothers and Sisters of Charity also has a domestic ex-pression. Members remain at home, meet in groups and attend regional and national gatherings. Yearly all come together at the Hermitage for a national gathering. The community, in both its domestic and monas-tic expressions, is Roman Catholic-based but ecumenical in scope. Though there are ten such communities throughout the world, Little Portion is the only community of its kind with canonical status in North America.

The breadth of its vision and endeavors in its monastic expression focuses upon integration. Little Portion Hermitage integrates the Benedictine and Franciscan traditions as well as the monastic tradi-tions of Eastern and Western Christianity. The Brothers and Sisters of Charity is a fully integrated community comprised of celibate broth-ers, celibate sisters, single individuals, family monastics with chil-dren. Likewise, within the monastic and prayer structure of the com-munity, there is an integration of silence and contemplation with spontaneous and charismatic prayer. Again, integration is the key in living styles. Celibate brothers and sisters and family monastics each have separate and distinct living areas, yet all come together in com-munity for prayer, meals and work.

The intent of the Brothers and Sisters of Charity is to live a rural, alternative, contemplative life-style as a witness and, through their integration of gender and marital status, solitude and community, contemplation and charismatic expressions, deliberately and con-sciously to choose to reconcile opposites. As John Michael, the "spir-itual father and general minister" of the community, says, "Integration is the key. The Cross reconciles opposites." He continues, "I see the community like a rope with strands. In looking at the rope, one still sees the individual strands."

Little Portion Hermitage is located in beautiful surroundings with its own structures adding to the quality of that natural beauty. Specific areas are designated for each of the distinct life choices of the members. All sections—the brothers' grove, the sisters' skete and the family area—are clustered around the common buildings used for worship, meals and work. The entire integrated monastery is patterned on the Celtic monasticism of Ireland, Scotland and much of England in the sixth and seventh centuries.

In the center of the valley are the common buildings, an architectural delight visually reminiscent of Russian styles. These buildings and surroundings include the chapel, the common center with kitchen and dining rooms, library, offices, porches, bell tower, rock gardens, cloister, prayer gardens, greenhouses, vegetable gardens and barn.

The Hermitage is not open to retreatants or people who may wish to come for periods of prayer and solitude. (Plans are being formed to build a small retreat center on the grounds in the near future so that retreatants may have access to the prayer and monastic rhythm of the community.) Nor does the Hermitage offer any specific programs of formation in prayer. Rather, one comes to the Hermitage to enter into the life and rhythm of the community. This is generally a preliminary step to joining as a member.

The community members practice the three evangelical counsels of poverty, chastity and obedience according to their state of life. Meals are taken in common, except for breakfast, with infants and family members alongside celibate brothers and sisters. Work is also shared in common. The community grows much of its own food and livestock for its own needs as well as sells some of its organically grown vegetables in the nearby resort restaurants of Eureka Springs.

John Michael is married and with his wife, Viola, lives in the community. They travel often as he performs concerts throughout the world. The proceeds from John Michael's concerts are used by the community in apostolic service to the poor and in establishing new communities, including a monastic community in Old Jerusalem, Israel, as well as domestic houses of prayer in Nebraska and New York.

The Brothers and Sisters of Charity do a considerable amount of apostolic work. Local ministries include the Little Portion Monastery Store, the Little Flower Clinic for the poor, the Little Portion Retreat and Training Center, weekly convalescent home visits, work with the St. Vincent de Paul Society, the Loaves and Fishes Food Bank, door-to-door visits, the cleaning of homes of the elderly and the disabled as well as local churches. The Brothers and Sisters also operate "Mercy Corps International," an agency that works with partner agencies to airlift emergency supplies to devastated areas of the world.

FEATURES FOR DISCERNMENT

- Fully integrated monastic community composed of vowed celibate men and women, single individuals, families with children and a domestic community who live in their own homes
- Integration of contemplative prayer with charismatic prayer, solitude with community, and contemplation with social action
- Only community of its kind with canonical status in North America
- Astoundingly beautiful architectural setting with biointensive gardens
- Traditional in faith orientation but highly innovative model
- Centered around a strong charismatic leader

DAILY SCHEDULE

6:45	Divine Office and praise
	Homily by John Michael or others
	Communion
7:00	Pick-up breakfast in silence
	Morning—soft silence, talking only in regard to work
	Morning hours: work in barn, garden, etc.
12:00	Angelus Prayer
	Noon (main) meal, seated, communal, social, not vegetarian
	Afternoon—no silence, but a quiet atmosphere
5:30	Evening Prayer—Divine Office (or some part) or sung praises
	Final Blessing
	(From morning until 5:30 p.m. monks sign up for one hour of adoration in chapel)
6:00	Pick-up supper, communal, social
	Wednesdays are fast days, homemade bread (delicious!) and water only

■ NEW CAMALDOLI HERMITAGE

Address: New Camaldoli Hermitage
  Big Sur, California 93920

Phone: 408-667-2456

Fax: 408-667-0209

Type of Contemplative Formation Model: Associate group of canonical community, retreats, hermitage

Founder: Camaldolese monks from Hermitage of Camaldoli in Tuscany, Italy

Director: Father Robert Hale, O.S.B. Cam. (Prior)

Guestmaster and Oblate Director: Father Isaiah Teichert, O.S.B. Cam.

Tradition: Christian, Roman Catholic, Benedictine, Camaldolese

Sources: The Christian monastic tradition, both Eastern and Western. More specifically, the Benedictine tradition, and within it, the Camaldolese tradition, which includes both community and solitude.

Start-up Date: 1958

Participant Profile: Retreatants come from all denominations, mostly Christian, but some from Asian traditions; some are without denomination. Retreatants include about an equal number of men and women. Married, single, divorced, widowed, clergy, religious, people of all ages (except children, to ensure quiet for others), come for retreat. The average length of stay for a retreat is three days, though there are some longer retreats of up to a month. Over ten thousand retreats have taken place at New Camaldoli since the start of the retreat house in 1961; many retreatants come back time and time again. Oblates presently number about three hundred from all over the United States but with the majority in California. Oblates are approximately fifty-five percent women and forty-five percent men. Retreatants and Oblates come basically in response to the magnetic attraction of a spiritual reality symbolized by and embodied in the monastic community and in its dwelling place.

Newsletter: Published quarterly, the *Camaldolese Tidings* communicates the news of the two Camaldolese monasteries in the United States: New Camaldoli Hermitage and Incarnation Monastery in Berkeley, California. Newsletters are distributed to Oblates, retreatants and friends.

Internet: *http://www.contemplation.com*

Programs: There are no structured retreats save for a half a dozen preached retreats during the year. Times for these retreats are published in the fall issue of the newsletter. Retreatants' and Oblates' experience consists in a participation in the spiritual life of the monks: liturgy, *lectio divina*, silent prayer and their own inner journeys.

Cost: There is no particular cost for the Oblate Program. Recommended donations for retreats are $45 per night if one stays at the retreat house; this includes meals and linens. If one stays at the trailer hermitages the cost is $55 per night or $335 per week.

In 1958 the first Camaldolese monastic community in the United States settled in the breathtaking, inspiring and rugged central coastal mountains (near Big Sur, California) overlooking the Pacific ocean. The natural beauty and solitude of the hermitage's eight hundred acres with views of woods and ocean support the contemplative way of life. There is now one other house for men in this country, Incarnation Priory in Berkeley, California. There is also a women's order in Windsor, New York.

The Camaldolese way of life is Benedictine in its origins and arose out of a reform movement in the eleventh century to revitalize the best of the communal and solitary dimensions of monastic life. Each of the twenty-five monks at New Camaldoli has his own monastic cottage where he spends the greater part of his day in contemplative solitude. The cottages, however, are situated near other buildings, which express the communal dimension of the monks' lives. The communal celebrations of the liturgy four times a day are held in the monks' chapel, a structure that conveys both the simplicity and directness of their chosen life-style. Other communal moments within the day include work, meals and recreation.

It is apparent that the monks are deeply involved not only in the practice of contemplation but also in sharing the fruits of contemplation. The monks support a retreat ministry wherein guests are invited to share in the silence and solitude of the community as well as their common prayer. There are nine short-term single retreat rooms, each with views overlooking the ocean, and five single trailers for longer occupancy. Retreats are not ordinarily structured and individuals make reservations for their own private retreats. Spiritual direction is available from one of the monks upon request. Retreatants are welcome to join in the liturgy and prayer of the monks including one half hour of silent meditation daily, following Vespers in the large chapel.

In the 1980's an Oblate program for lay women and men was started in order to include non-monks as part of an extended Camaldolese family. There are about three hundred Oblates in the United States, both men and women, most of whom are in California. As explained in the Oblate Rule, "Camaldolese Benedictine Oblates are a group of Christians who experience an attraction of the Holy Spirit to deep prayer, and experience a bond of friendship with our monastic community and its long spiritual tradition.... Oblates are extended members of the Camaldolese Benedictine family."

Formation of a Camaldolese Oblate begins with a six-month probation period during which the candidate studies and prays over the Rule for Oblates to "see how well it 'fits' and to discern the Spirit's movement in the candidate's life." There is a formal ceremony for the reception of an Oblate, usually held at New Camaldoli Hermitage. During the initial formation period there is a list of recommended readings and tapes including Camaldolese authors, Thomas Merton, Father Bede Griffiths, the sayings of the desert fathers; a broad and deep list to enrich one's knowledge of prayer and contemplation as a layperson.

Oblates are asked to write or meet once a year with the Oblate chaplain as a means of keeping in touch physically and spiritually. They are asked to celebrate Eucharist weekly at least and encouraged to practice *lectio divina* (particularly the meditative reading of Scripture) and to pray various Hours of the Divine Office when possible. They are also encouraged to spend daily time (twenty minutes twice a day, if possible) in silent meditation using the Jesus Prayer, Centering Prayer, Christian Meditation and so on. Silence and solitude are to be included in some way if possible in the daily lives of the Oblates.

One doesn't need to be in the Oblate program, or become an Oblate, to take advantage of the richness New Camaldoli has to offer. As Father Bruno Barnhart pointed out, "new models are needed by lay contemplatives," so perhaps it is not necessary or even always fitting for lay men and women seeking deeper contemplation to try to fit their spiritual lives into a quasi-monastic model. Contact with wisdom inherent in such a monastic order need not take such a formal commitment, though it may give more of a sense of sharing and community than is possible otherwise.

The opportunities offered for both retreatants and Oblates at New Camaldoli Hermitage seem some of the deepest and richest offerings for those who wish to go much deeper into contemplative prayer. As Father Bruno indicates, "The value of this site is in the monastic contemplative tradition, particularly in its simple and solitary forms. This expression is nested, however, within a natural setting which has a special power." The experience of New Camaldoi Hermitage is open to contemplatives at all stages of the journey. Spiritual direction is available when needed. A wonderful bookstore/gift shop offers significant reading material and some of the artistic creations of the monks.

FEATURES FOR DISCERNMENT

- Breathtaking natural setting overlooking Pacific Ocean
- Eremetical (hermit) monastic community with emphasis on solitude
- Comfortable but not rigid silence
- Unstructured private retreats with optional involvement in community prayer
- Simply structured Oblate program available
- Worthwhile formative experience for the contemplative in any stage of development

■ SECULAR ORDER OF DISCALCED CARMELITES

Address: OCDS Central Office
Western Province, P.O. Box 3079
San Jose, California 95156-3079

Phone: 408-251-1361

Type of Contemplative Model: Secular Order, international network, retreats, courses, workshops, local support groups

Founder: General Superior of Order

Director: Father Michael Buckley, O.C.D.

Tradition: Christian, Roman Catholic, Carmelite

Sources: Teresa of Avila, John of the Cross, Therese of Lisieux

Start-up Date: 1924 for Western Province, U.S.A.

Participant Profile: Roman Catholic in orientation and membership. In the Western Province a total of 2,031 members, a growth of nearly fourteen percent since 1996. Membership is eighty percent women, twenty percent men. Open to Catholic men and women eighteen years of age and older.

Newsletter: A provincial newsletter is published four times a year for members of the Secular Order in the Western Province. Father Michael Buckley writes the newsletter for the Western Province. The Eastern and Central Provinces also publish newsletters for their members.

Programs: Members attend monthly meetings on the local level. National Congresses are assembled every three years for members of all of the three Provinces (Eastern, Central and Western); International Congresses are held periodically.

Cost: None to be a member.

For centuries many Catholic lay men and women have felt themselves drawn to a closer association with a particular religious order because of a resonance with its ideals and/or spirituality and as a way of supporting and nourishing their own call to holiness in the world. Even today monastic orders have their oblate programs which serve this purpose while the Mendicant Orders have their secular orders. Members of the Discalced Carmelite Secular Order, like members of other secular orders, "try to develop their spiritual life by a closer association with the spirituality of the religious order to which they are attracted" (*Information Pamphlet, Secular Order of Discalced Carmelites*).

According to Father Michael Buckley, O.C.D., delegate provincial for the western province of the Secular Carmelites, "the Carmelite Secular Order shares in fraternal communion with the Order, and depends on us for its ideals, charism." In the Western Province there are thirty fully constituted communities with 1,540 members from Seattle to Santa Fe. There are thirteen groups (188 members) on the way to being established. There are also three study groups totalling twenty-five, as well as 227 lay people in the province who are isolated members and not joined to a particular group.

All members have a formation period of five years. In the first two years prior to first promises, candidates attend twenty-four classes on the spiritual life with readings from Saint John of the Cross and Saint Teresa of Avila, two of the Order's most renowned saints. The next three years prior to final promises are filled with an additional thirty-six classes, all by way of preparation for living as a Secular Carmelite in the world. After the completion of the five years of formation, members make a definitive promise to "tend toward evangelical perfection in the spirit of the evangelical counsels of chastity, poverty, obedience, and of the Beatitudes" (*Secular Order Rule*).

The daily duties of a Secular Carmelite include one half-hour of meditation or solitary prayer daily, recitation of some of the Hours from the Divine Office, observance of some of the obligations of the Carmelite feasts and attendance at daily Mass as often as possible.

Secular Carmelites ordinarily belong to a group formed on the local level. For these established groups there are monthly meetings. It is necessary for a Carmelite spiritual assistant, a priest, to be present at some part of each meeting, at council meetings and at ceremonies. The monthly meetings generally tie in with the local church. Formation may consist of reading from some of the Carmelite spiritual classics.

In regard to contemplative prayer, it seems Father Buckley doesn't speak much about "passive contemplation," but rather encourages Secular Carmelites in ways of more active meditation and affective prayer forms. As to benefits for themselves (as Secular Carmelites) and for the Church, Father Buckley feels membership in the Secular Order "would give people a reference point to God and His creation. It would keep conscious in their [members'] lives their experience of God. [Secular Carmelites] would also have a good effect on everyone with whom they came in contact. They would realize they are sons and daughters of the Church...which would be of great effect on the Church."

All three regions or provinces in the United States may not operate with the same spiritual goals and approaches to secular formation as the Western Province. There is no doubt a unity of organization and purpose among the provinces. Only the Western Province fell within the scope of this study.

FEATURES FOR DISCERNMENT

- Traditional faith orientation
- Daily prayer commitment and special observance of Carmelite feasts
- Monthly local meetings and tri-annual national congress
- Strong emphasis on priestly presence at meetings
- Highly structured program in the context of Carmelite spirituality

■ LEBH SHOMEA HOUSE OF PRAYER

Address: La Parra Ranch
P.O. Box 9
Sarita, Texas 78385-0009

Phone: 361-294-5369

Fax: 361-294-5791

Type of Contemplative Formation Model: Private and directed retreats, courses and workshops on spirituality, long-term residential opportunities, individual dwellings and hermitages are available.

Founder: Francis Kelly Nemeck, O.M.I., and Marie Theresa Coombs, hermit

Tradition: Christian, Roman Catholic

Sources: Christian antiquity, Scripture, Eastern and Western mystical traditions

Start-up Date: 1973

Participant Profile: Most people coming to Lebh Shomea are Roman Catholic, but there are people from other denominations including Episcopalians, Lutherans and Methodists, as well as some without any formal religious affiliation. All who come are consciously on a spiritual quest. The house of prayer is open year-round to men and women of all ages.

Programs: Guests participate in the contemplative-eremetical life of the House of Prayer, entering into the freedom and creativity of solitude and silence. All are invited to share in daily Eucharist, and spiritual direction is available to guests upon request. There is an annual desert experience of forty days and nights from June 21 to July 31, a more structured program, that includes a daily conference on prayer and the spiritual life. Lebh Shomea is also a school of prayer offering two programs in the study of the theology of Christian spirituality leading to a Certificate of Studies or academic credit through the Oblate School of Theology, San Antonio, Texas.

Cost: $33 per day with reduced rates the longer you stay

"Give your servant a listening heart (*Lebh Shomea*) so as to be able to discern..." (1 Kings 3:9). This Hebrew phrase seems to sum up both the history and spiritual mission of Lebh Shomea House of Prayer near Sarita, Texas. It may also express the desires of those guests who come to this house of prayer.

Located on La Parra Ranch, nearly halfway between Corpus Christi and Brownsville, Texas, the present location of Lebh Shomea was formerly ranch land in the nineteenth century. The Missionary Oblates of Mary Immaculate had met the ranch owners, the Kenedys, in the mid 1800's as the priests traveled up and down the coast ministering to the Hispanic population. The Kenedys were wealthy landowners with over two hundred hired hands. The priests would stop at the ranch for a week or ten days after arduous horseback travel. Nearly one hundred years later, in 1961, Sarita Kenedy East died childless. Remembering her mother's love for the Missionary Oblates, she willed a large portion of La Parra Ranch, including her own house and beach property, to the Order. Perhaps this was the first "listening heart."

For twelve years the Oblates used this property as a novitiate for their Southern United States Province until, as religious vocations decreased, the candidates for the Order were sent to a centralized novitiate in Godfrey, Illinois.

In June 1973, the property was designated by the Order as a house of prayer. A Missionary Oblate, Father Herve Marcoux, its first director, suggested both the name and the contemplative thrust for Lebh Shomea. In November of 1973 Father Kelly Nemeck, O.M.I., joined the community and in March 1974, Sister Marie Theresa Coombs joined the core community. Many ideas were proposed and attempted for programs for guests. But the core community discerned, with "listening hearts," that due in part to the remoteness and seclusion of the ranch, silence and solitude and an eremetical (hermit) contemplative thrust were the directions to be followed. That has remained the spirit of the house of prayer to this day.

In the early 1980's a "school of prayer" was also established offering a Certificate of Studies and, in conjunction with the Oblate School of Theology in San Antonio, offering a Practicum in Spirituality for candidates of various degree programs.

Today, though Lebh Shomea is still owned by the Missionary Oblates who sponsor it, a core community of three—Father Kelly Nemeck, Sister Marie Coombs and Sister Maria Meister—collectively and collegially handle the internal functions, the practical decisions and the spiritual discernment of the house of prayer. The two women of the core community are canonically recognized hermits.

One hundred acres is used for Lebh Shomea house of prayer with thirty buildings on this property. There are twelve solitary dwellings;

four of the twelve are set up for married couples. There are three guest hermitages: two for overnight stays and one day hermitage. The original house of Sarita Kenedy East, called the "Big House," has twelve guest rooms, a dining area for guests and a library housing thirty thousand volumes, including everything from the usual biblical, patristic and spiritual classics to Byzantine, Islamic, Judaic, Middle Eastern, Oriental and Russian spirituality studies.

Every guest at Lebh Shomea is considered a part of the community. As Sister Marie Coombs explains, "When one comes here, one enters into community. The model for community is the Trinity. The core community is the permanent base, but the guests make up an important part of the community." She adds, "Silence is not 'me and God' but a way of being present to each other in God."

Because of the eremetical thrust of Lebh Shomea, guests observe silence constantly even during meals in common. There is no schedule except for the daily celebration of Eucharist in which all are encouraged to participate. Each guest upon arriving at the house of prayer meets with a member of the core community. The accent is on the individual person with his or her needs and desires. The charism of "the listening heart" calls for a respect for the movement of the Spirit in each individual sharing in this community for whatever length of time. Individual spiritual direction is available and ongoing if a guest so desires. If not, one is left alone to dwell in silence and solitude.

Annually, from June 21 to July 31, there is a desert experience, lasting forty days and nights, for six to fifteen people, which includes a daily conference on prayer and the spiritual life. It is a guided and more structured experience than usual and, as one of the core members remarked, "a greater sense of community forms based on the group."

Near the Big House is the Kenedy family chapel, a lovely, exquisitely designed building in beautiful condition dating back to 1897. Sunday liturgy is held here for the community of Lebh Shomea as well as friends in the area.

The solitary dwellings are rather new, solidly built of brick, each with its own bedroom with bed and desk, storage room, bath and shower, and small oratory. Each dwelling also has a small screened porch. Paths connect dwellings to the main paths which converge at the Big House, the center of the one-hundred-acre complex. The additional one thousand acres are rented for grazing land.

The entire property is also a wildlife refuge, so wild turkey, armadillos, rabbits, deer, javelina and an occasional vulture wander to and fro past the hermitages. The landscape around the estate, and the house itself, is physically magnificent. As one of the core members stated, "We are incarnationally oriented, we value nature. Nature is one of the things that touches people the most." As a result, a developing part of the vision of Lebh Shomea has been that of welcoming creative expression. There is a community building housing photography, poetry and crafts that have emerged from guests' experiences of silence and solitude.

The core community of Lebh Shomea define themselves as a house of prayer with their foremost obligation to secure as much solitude, time for personal prayer and study as is necessary "for an adequate response to God's call." Their apostolate is "that of being contemplative and eremetical to those who are contemplatively and eremetically inclined." It is, very simply, "a presence: here I am," or as Teilhard de Chardin would say, "being with Christ at the heart of the world." Both Father Nemeck and Sister Marie Coombs have written eight to ten books on the spiritual journey, contemplation and/or spiritual direction, with five of these books translated into Spanish.

Though the silence and solitude are somewhat austere, the advantages of being plunged into it are many, especially with the scholarly and experienced core community available for spiritual direction and guidance. The library offers tremendous opportunities for study on contemplation and the great classics of spirituality. For a serious seeker on the contemplative path, Lebh Shomea could offer opportunities not available anywhere else. There are few houses of prayer in the United States with an eremetical thrust and such opportunity for scholarly study. It would require someone who is both well balanced and serious minded, though, to integrate a long stay here.

FEATURES FOR DISCERNMENT

- Eremetical model with high degree of silence and solitude
- Highly unstructured
- Remote location—not easily accessible—some restricted areas
- Beautifully landscaped grounds
- Unique library and school of prayer with optional college credit or certification
- Wildlife refuge
- Long-term stable core community
- Only communal prayer is daily Roman Catholic Eucharist

■ CISTERCIAN LAY CONTEMPLATIVES

Address: P.O. Box 317844
　　　　　Cincinnati, Ohio 45231

Phone: 513-522-8240

Type of Contemplative Formation Model: Local support groups, national network

Founder: Core Group (eight people) including monk of Gethsemani

Abbey Contact Person: Michael Johnson

Tradition: Christian, Roman Catholic, Benedictine Cistercian

Sources: Cistercian/Benedictine tradition, Rule of St. Benedict

Start-up Date: 1989

Participant Profile: The majority of members are Roman Catholic, but there is an openness to other Christian denominations. Members are usually over thirty years of age with a ratio of sixty percent men and forty percent women. The membership consists of married and single people. People join the Cistercian Lay Contemplatives (CLC) because they are seeking connectedness, support, spiritual companioning. Approximately eighty people have participated as Cistercian Lay Contemplatives since its founding.

Newsletter: A national newsletter is published quarterly and distributed among eighty to one hundred persons.

Programs: Local groups meet monthly and gather three times a year for a day of prayer at the Abbey of Gethsemani in Kentucky. There is also an annual retreat at Gethsemani Abbey and Holy Spirit Abbey in Georgia.

Cost: $5 annual subscription to CLC newsletter

Cistercian Lay Contemplatives define themselves as "ordinary Christian men and women who have formed an association of support in their effort to live a contemplative life at the Abbey of Gethsemani in Kentucky for several years." The group gathered several times at the Abbey and developed a Plan of Life, a suggested guide for living a contemplative spirituality in one's ordinary lifestyle. The Plan of Life, rooted in the Cistercian (Trappist) and Benedictine charism and monastic disciplines "gives expression to the desire of laity who want to experience the richness of Cistercian spirituality within the context of the secular lifestyle." The major elements discussed in the Plan of Life are prayer, work, study, silence, solitude, simplicity and service/ministry. Each point of the Plan is developed in the light of centuries of Cistercian experience, yet modified and integrated into today's life-style for lay people.

There is not a structured formation process for CLC associates. There is, however, a recommended reading list providing information and guidance on Benedictine and Cistercian history and spirituality as well as contemplative prayer and the contemplative dimension of life.

There are currently three local communities of Cistercian Lay Contemplatives in Louisville, Kentucky, in Bardstown, Kentucky, and in Cincinnati, Ohio. A small group is beginning to form in Washington, D.C., and there is a desire to begin a group in Wilmington, Delaware. All local groups come together three times a year for a day of prayer at the Abbey of Gethsemani. In addition, they meet for an annual retreat at the Abbey. There are currently sixty-five to seventy CLC members.

Locally, each group meets monthly. Though the format differs with each group, an example of what occurs at such meetings is illustrated by the meetings of the Cincinnati branch of CLC. The Cincinnati branch meets the first Saturday of each month in a parish hall (smaller local groups meet in members' homes) for morning prayer, sharing over breakfast, then a prayer service or discussion. Some months the Enneagram tapes of Father Richard Rohr have been studied. Currently one group is discussing *Spirituality for Everyday Living* by Brian Taylor, a contemporary adaptation of the Rule of St. Benedict.

It is important to note that, although CLC had its origins with a group who met at the Abbey of Gethsemani and has supportive unofficial ties with some monks of the Abbey, CLC does not have any official recognition or approval by the Abbey of Gethsemani or any Cistercian monastic community. "CLC is an independent association of those who feel attracted to the Benedictine/Cistercian tradition as a basis for living a contemplative spirituality in the non-monastic setting of our ordinary lives," says Michael Johnson, the national contact person for CLC. He says that CLC is a broader approach than merely being connected to a specific monastery; CLC is not a third order nor does it seek canonical recognition in any way. As another member notes, "The original intent was, for those who felt drawn contemplatively, simply to be a network, to share with one another."

Due to the loosely knit or unstructured approach of the association, members do not see themselves as "experts" in regard to spiritual guidance. They see themselves as having a common interest and thus encourage one another in spiritual reading and spiritual companioning. The heart of the CLC program, members feel, is in the practice of living out the elements of the Plan of Life.

Participants learn of CLC through word of mouth and newsletters in reading rooms of Cistercian retreat houses. The only cost involved in becoming a member is a $5 annual subscription fee to the CLC newsletter. The newsletter keeps members in touch, and the meetings and retreats allow them to share with those on a similar path. That sharing can be a great nourishment and encouragement toward growing deeper into the contemplative dimension.

Brother Paul Quenon of the Abbey of Gethsemani is currently the spiritual advisor to CLC, replacing Father Michael Casagram, who is out of the country on assignment. Father Michael spoke of the Abbey's role in CLC: "We see ourselves at the Abbey as providing a climate in which participants in the program are encouraged to live the Plan and share their experience. We also open our place for retreats and meetings that are occasionally held here."

Though CLC is loosely structured and probably would require self-motivation and some previously developed spiritual disciplines on the part of the member, it would provide a welcome association and network for those laypersons attracted to the Cistercian tradition of contemplative spirituality. Though it is an independent lay association, its physical proximity to a Cistercian monastery undoubtedly helps provide focus and richness to its vision and practices. The CLC Plan of Life and reading list offer guidance and structure for lay men and women desiring to live out the contemplative dimension of their lives in the world.

FEATURES FOR DISCERNMENT

- Lay association with adapted Plan of Life based on Cistercian/Benedictine spirituality
- Unofficial connection with Abbey of Gethsemani in Kentucky
- Loosely structured
- Monthly meetings, three days of prayer at Gethsemani as well as annual retreat
- Occasional national meetings with other Cistercian Lay Associates

■ SHALEM INSTITUTE FOR SPIRITUAL FORMATION

Address: 5430 Grosvenor Lane
Bethesda, Maryland 20814

Phone: 301-897-7334

Fax: 301-897-3719

Type of Contemplative Formation Model: Retreats, courses, workshops, home study programs with intensives

Founder: Rev. Dr. Tilden Edwards

Director: Rev. Dr. Tilden Edwards

Tradition: Christian contemplative with occasional influence from Asian contemplative traditions, especially Mahayana Buddhist, adapted for a Christian context

Sources: John of the Cross, Teresa of Avila, the medieval mystics, the Desert Fathers, Scripture

Start-up Date: 1973

Participant Profile: An average of seven to ten Christian denominational backgrounds can be found in a typical Shalem group; eight denominations are represented on the staff. Approximately seventy-five percent of participants in programs are women, twenty-five percent men, with ages ranging mostly between thirty and seventy. People come to Shalem's offerings mainly because they are hungering for the "more" of God. Their average length of stay can be anywhere from one day to two years depending upon the program in which they are participating. Some people continue in different programs over many years. The majority of people who attend Shalem's offerings are married but as many as thirty-five percent are not.

Newsletter: *The Shalem News* is published four times a year and is offered free for two years and then usually in exchange for a contribution to Shalem's Annual Fund.

Internet: *http//www.shalem.org*

Programs: Request annual program guide for complete list of current annual events.

Cost: Ranges from free to $6,000+ depending upon the program.

In the Shalem Institute for Spiritual Formation we find an ecumenical organization whose primary focus is to offer programs for lay Christian contemplative formation. Founded in 1973, Shalem has fostered contemplative presence and understanding through its numerous and varied programs and offerings each year. Its current staff of eight full-time and twenty-five part-time administrative and program staff comprise different religious backgrounds and a varied vocational mix, but all are committed, as founder and director Tilden Edwards declares, "to a shared intention of immediate, contemplative presence for God, in a unique range of programmatic offerings."

Shalem offers some long-term as well as short-term programs. The long-term offerings include a two-year spiritual guidance program designed for those engaged in the ministry of spiritual direction; a one-year group leaders program for leaders of short- and long-term contemplative spiritual formation groups; a one-year program for group spiritual directors; an eighteen-month personal spiritual deepening program for those seeking a contemplative grounding within the context of daily life; and a two-year "Soul of the Executive" program for executives in both profit and nonprofit organizations. All of the long-term programs include some residential activities at Shalem as well as work at home.

In addition to its long-term programs, Shalem offers a series of retreats, workshops, weekly and monthly groups, special events, quiet days and pilgrimages. Offerings include everything from workshops on the dark night of the soul to a Michigan Wilderness Retreat. An annual program guide lists each of the Institute's offerings for the year, along with descriptions of each particular event. A registration form accompanies each of the program offerings.

The Institute's Center, located on Grosvenor Lane in Bethesda, Maryland, is used as a gathering place for Shalem's nonresidential events. Many of the monthly and weekly group sessions are held in the Shalem Meditation Room at this site. Shalem's Center also houses a spirituality library that is available as a resource to any seeker. Although the Center is actually located in an office complex (housing the administrative offices of Shalem), the environment of lovely trees on the grounds of the Renewable Natural Resources Center surrounding the office buildings, as well as the tasteful interior design of the Shalem office complex, contribute to creating an atmosphere of peace and serenity within its walls.

Most of the longer residential programs offered by the Institute are held at Bon Secours Spiritual Center in Marriottsville, Maryland. The retreat center, located in the Maryland countryside on three hundred acres of rolling hills, offers ample accommodations for Shalem's extended programs, workshops and retreats, though the retreat center environment is somewhat busy and institutional. Other sites in the Baltimore and Washington, D.C., areas, such as the Washington National Cathedral and Holy Trinity Retreat Center, are occasionally selected for Shalem's special events.

There is exposure to a broad range of contemplative traditions and practices within Shalem's many and varied programs. Primarily there is the influence of the Christian contemplative tradition as expressed in John of the Cross, Teresa of Avila, the medieval mystics, the desert fathers and Scripture. Also there is occasional exposure to Asian contemplative traditions adapted for a Christian context. No one method of contemplative prayer is emphasized but, as Tilden Edwards observed, "we do emphasize immediate presence/givenness to God through whatever method is offered, and assume a great divine/human intimacy."

The *Shalem News*, published three times a year, offers its readers a series of insightful articles authored by members of the Institute's staff. As the newsletter itself indicates, *Shalem News* "provides groundings, findings, direction and new ideas about spiritual formation." In addition, there is a calendar of upcoming events and programs as well as an opportunity to order spiritual books and tapes authored by members of the Institute's staff.

Staff members are not only academically prepared for their ministry but also oriented toward the practice of contemplative living in their own lives. Shalem can boast of many outstanding program leaders, including Gerald May, author of *Addiction and Grace* and *The Awakened Heart* and many other books and articles on the relationship between spirituality and psychology. Shalem's Executive Director, Tilden Edwards, is also a recognized author of numerous books on spirituality, including *Sabbath Time* and *Living in the Presence*. Sister Rose Mary Dougherty is the author of both the book and videotape *Group Spiritual Direction*.

The Institute's programs are well organized, academically sound and well grounded in the Christian contemplative tradition. Emphasis within the programs is upon experience, upon the practice of the contemplative life. Beginners in the spiritual life as well as those who are more advanced will be able to find program offerings that will nurture their own individual development.

FEATURES FOR DISCERNMENT

- Primary focus on lay contemplative formation
- Offers a wide range of outstanding programs
- Staff includes well-known spiritual leaders and authors personally involved in contemplative practice
- Utilizes methods primarily from Christian contemplative traditions but also adapts methods from Eastern traditions
- Offers unique home study programs
- Well-developed ecumenical thrust

■ ACADEMY FOR SPIRITUAL FORMATION

Address: 1908 Grand Ave.
Box 189
Nashville, Tennessee 37202

Phone: 615-340-7232

Type of Contemplative Formation Model: Courses, support groups

Founder: Rev. Danny E. Morris

Director: Rev. Jerry Haas

Tradition: A broad sweep of Christian spirituality, but touches Hebrew, Orthodox, Roman Catholic and Wesleyan spiritualities

Sources: Scripture, Protestant and Roman Catholic spiritualities

Start-up Date: May 1983

Participant Profile: Participants are often United Methodists, but the program aims for a Christian ecumenical inclusiveness. Faculty is a broad mix of mainline Judeo-Christian traditions. Participants are about forty-five percent women and fifty-five percent men, of all ages but mainly from the late thirties to the late sixties. Over seven hundred men and women have participated in the more intense two-year academy with more than four thousand in the single five-day modules. Married and single laity as well as clergy have participated in the program.

Newsletter: *Academy Forum*

Programs: A core two-year program divided into quarterly (eight) five-day residency periods with follow-up work in between. The residency programs are held at one of three special sites. A five-day module of the core program is currently held in fifteen to twenty states nationwide. There are also Academy expansion courses focusing on spirituality in the African-American tradition and three-year covenant communities.

Cost: About $4,400 plus travel and books for the two-year Academy. Interested persons are encouraged to apply. If cost is a problem, the Academy helps work out financial solutions.

"Where do lay persons go to specialize in their faith journey? Where do clergy go to sharpen the focus of spirituality in their ministry, which they are now more likely open to than when they were in seminary?" These questions formed the heart of a search for a Methodist clergyman, the Reverend Danny E. Morris, in 1981. Working with twenty consultants in a wide range of Christian denominational and theological positions through a year of searching, four months of study leave, and a year and a half of integration and insight, Danny developed the ideas for the Academy for Spiritual Formation. The Academy began in May 1983, with well-known Catholic, Protestant and Quaker theologians, among others, helping to finalize the program. It is sponsored by the Upper Room, a department of the board of discipleship of the United Methodist Church, with the founder, Danny Morris, as executive director. The stated purpose of the Academy is "to provide an in-depth and comprehensive experience in spiritual formation for lay and clergy who are highly motivated in their sense of call to follow Christ and serve the Church and the world."

The core two-year residency program consists of sixteen courses addressing seven major areas offered in quarterly five-day residency periods. These are set within an almost monastic schedule of prayer, study, silence, worship and covenant support groups. Participants are encouraged and instructed in healthy diet and exercise as well as spiritual friending and regular journaling.

The seven "curriculum essentials" include the place and use of Scripture in spiritual formation; models of spirituality; instruction in spiritual discipline; spirituality, psychology and inner healing; historical framework for spiritual formation; servanthood; the role of the Church in spiritual formation. Each area uses impressive texts and readings.

Participants (up to fifty-six for each two-year academy) go to one of three locations in the United States for all the intensives of their two-year program. There have been thirteen two-year academies since its formation with over six hundred people having completed the program. It is open to any man or woman, lay or clergy, and is ecumenical in participation as well as content.

Each Academy is led by a five-member team who themselves have completed a two-year Academy and are chosen for specific leadership abilities and gifts that emerge. There is also an adjunct faculty (a rotating faculty of two per session) who are in residence with participants each session. The adjunct faculty, outstanding Judeo-Christian leaders and nationally known spiritual teachers, provide specialized content stipulated by the curriculum.

The curriculum is a structured, organized, unchanging program of one morning and afternoon session. Following the morning and afternoon curriculum, a small bell is rung to signify silence. There is an hour of total silence as participants leave for solitude, prayer and reflection. There is also community silence following night prayer until morning prayer the next day.

Participants are nurtured in the Spirit through their study and prayer, through silence, through optional contemplative experiences such as centering prayer, and through their personal and community worship. They are encouraged to participate in spiritual guidance, to keep a journal and to be a "spiritual friend" to another person.

One of the most vital components of the Academy is the establishment of covenant groups. Participants are divided into groups of eight members each who meet nightly for one and a half hours during the intensives and remain as a group for the duration of their Academy. Covenant groups meet to "process the day, share their journeys, and to provide a setting for group spiritual guidance." For the first covenant meeting a convenor (or leader) from the leadership team always shares the story of "The Rabbi's Gift" from *The Different Drum*, by M. Scott Peck. Then the group is left to itself and a convenor is chosen from the group. That convenor helps to open and close daily covenant group meetings and helps to provide some hospitality and leadership for each group. Convenors (of each group) meet over breakfast each day to share group issues and concerns with the leadership team and receive community guidance.

Participants make and sign a personal covenant each year, a commitment that focuses them. The first year addresses their inner life, perhaps a covenant to keep a spiritual journal or pray daily. The second-year covenant pertains to their outer life and world, as part of bearing witness. Sometimes participants have written articles or books or launched a project in their local church community. The spiritual magazine *Weavings* came out of such a covenant made at one of the two-year academies.

Though the Academy is not overtly contemplative in purpose, a definite contemplative thread runs through the entire program and is felt in the silence, the communal prayer, the orderliness and hospitality of the leadership team. There is talk and spontaneous enjoyment in the meals and times of sharing, but all seems to come out of a sense of spaciousness and grace, a centeredness. Much of this may have to do with the well-organized format. But, more than that, there is an atmosphere of wholeness and integrity to the program that seems to emanate from a deep contemplative center, from the Spirit. The beautiful settings and appropriate physical environments add to this sense.

The physical environment seems quite important for there is an intentional sense of a monastic rhythm, a contemplative rhythm throughout each day. The leadership team feels a natural setting conducive to solitude and simplicity, with religious symbols that evoke deeper spiritual dimensions, is an ideal site for an Academy.

Those interested in attending a two-year Academy must fill out an application and provide a short essay and three references. A personal interview may be requested.

As a result of the success of the two-year Academy, several expansion or spin-off programs have evolved. A five-day Academy has developed which is one five-day module of the two-year Academy. Fifteen to twenty states have held a five-day Academy, each sponsored by the Upper Room. Unlike the two-year Academy which is one time only, a person may attend multiple five-day academies. These five-day residential programs have become seed beds for two-year academies. Another spin-off has been a three-year covenant model in which participants meet four times a year for a weekend with one teaching staff person.

The Academy for Spiritual Formation and the spiritual fruits produced seem today to be a grace-filled answer to that Methodist clergyman's deep searching quest for "where do lay persons go to specialize in their faith journey? where do clergy go?" They now go to the Academy for Spiritual Formation. Father Edward Farrell, a Catholic priest and well-known author on prayer and spirituality, states that it is the best two-year program of its type anywhere in the world.

FEATURES FOR DISCERNMENT

- Faith orientation primarily United Methodist but draws upon all Judeo-Christian traditions
- Combines intensives with at-home practices
- Daily schedule modeled on monastic rhythm
- Highly structured program
- Daily Eucharist
- Participants honor balance between solitude and community
- Emphasizes balance of mind, body and spirit
- Unique concept of covenant groups which is vital dimension of program
- Contemplative formation one dimension of total spiritual formation program

SAMPLE SCHEDULE

Days One to Four

7:30-8:00	Morning Prayer
8:00	Breakfast
9:00-10:00	Curriculum I
10:00-11:00	Silence and solitude for prayer and reflection
11:00-11:30	Plenary discussion with faculty
12:00	Lunch
2:30-3:30	Curriculum II
3:30-4:30	Silence and solitude for prayer and reflection
4:30-5:00	Plenary discussion with faculty
5:15-6:00	Evening Prayer/Eucharist
6:00	Dinner
7:45-9:15	Covenant Groups
9:30-9:45	Night Prayer
	Silence observed in rooms and halls during the night until Morning Prayer

Day Five

7:00	Morning Prayer
7:30	Breakfast
8:00-9:00	Curriculum I
9:00-9:15	Break
9:15-10:15	Curriculum II

10:30	Eucharist
12:00	Lunch

Note: Schedule provides each faculty person with four teaching sessions, four reaction sessions and one session on Day Five for summing up the week.

The Leadership Team may call for a forty-five minute period for community building (or critiquing) either after lunch or after dinner at one or more sessions.

■ FELLOWSHIP OF THE HOLY TRINITY

Address: c/o St. Timothy's Episcopal Church
2575 Parkway Drive
Winston-Salem, North Carolina 27103

Phone: 910-765-0294

Type of Contemplative Formation Model: Community with formal and informal support networks

Founder: Dr. Beatrice Bruteau

Director: Kristin Farmer

Tradition: Christian, Benedictine; Vedanta; science

Sources: Vedantic, Judaic, Platonic, Buddhist, Christian, humanistic, scientific, *Foundations of Mysticism, World Spirituality, Mysteries of Life and the Universe, What is Life?, Science and Spirit, The Music of Man, The Creative Impulse, God's Ecstasy,* Benedictine monasticism with Gregorian office

Start-up Date: March 1993

Participant Profile: Persons of any denomination are welcome in the Fellowship. To date, members include Episcopalians, Roman Catholics and Baptists. Approximately thirty-six percent are men, sixty-four percent women. Members range in age from thirty-five to eighty. People attracted to the Fellowship are already engaged in contemplative life and desire community life and further instruction. The present membership has mostly completed the fifth year of formation. There are a number of novices and associates. Members are self-supporting. Membership is open to married and single people.

Programs: A five-year formation program leading into acceptance into the community.

Cost: No fees, dues. Self-maintenance, purchase of habit, books, undisclosed donations to small treasury to cover costs of invited teachers on occasion.

A few years ago the concept of a university without walls took the benefit of higher learning beyond its institutional framework and made it accessible to ordinary people in their own environment. In like manner the Fellowship of the Holy Trinity may be said to be a monastery without walls that makes the values of monastic life available to people who remain in their own homes. The Fellowship was founded in 1993 by Beatrice Bruteau. She recognized that the riches of the monastic tradition could be made accessible to the laity without disrupting their family lives and/or previous commitments. The Fellowship, moreover, would provide a means of spiritual support to contemplatives in the world who oftentimes found themselves very much alone in their quest for God.

Based upon the Benedictine form of monasticism, the Fellowship forms its own pattern of community influenced by its "unique charisms of ecumenicity and secularity." The Benedictine influence is apparent in the Fellowship's organizational structure and its use of the Benedictine Rule and practices. Practices include "chanting the Divine Office in choir, doing one's work as worship, giving oneself to study and creative expressions of various sorts (literature, art, music), keeping silence as feasible in one's state of life."

Currently, while remaining open to all other denominations, the community holds an ecumenical mixture of Episcopalians, Roman Catholics and Baptists. All current community members are or have been married. The Fellowship describes itself as an "extended community of people living in their own homes, attending to their respective obligations of work and family, who undertake a life of prayer and meditation, study and community sharing."

The Fellowship has a five-year scholarly and intense formation program that gives its community members a common background in the ideals of monasticism, methods of meditation, the interpretation of the Bible for contemplative life, Christian and non-Christian mysticism, science and the arts. Dr. Beatrice Bruteau originally held the position of spiritual guide and is responsible for much of the teaching. Beatrice holds a Ph.D. in philosophy from Fordham University. She has a background of studies with both the Ramakrishna Order and the Catholic Church. She is a well-known author and lecturer on contemplative life and prayer.

The outward structure of the formation process at the Fellowship is similar to the stages of formation encountered in religious communities with its progression from an aspirant level (three months) through postulancy (six to nine months), novitiate (one year) and juniorate (three years) levels to profession. Members make a professed commitment to live out this particular expression of monastic life at the conclusion of their formation period. Charter members have completed their formation, made their profession and elected a new Guide, Kristin Farmer. Guides serve five-year terms.

Professed members of the Fellowship wear a white alb with an orange scapular at community functions such as Vespers. The white garment is reminiscent of one's baptismal robe and reminds members of their total immersion in Christ. The orange scapular symbolizes both the soil of the earth and the flame of divine aspiration. It marks the community's tie to the monastic traditions of Hinduism and Buddhism.

Monthly chapter meetings and study meetings are an essential part of the community's life. Members convene for a common meal, instruction, Vespers and sharing.

In its six years of existence, the Fellowship of the Holy Trinity has attracted fourteen members to its community life and practice in two locations, North Carolina and Washington, D.C. Holy Trinity provides a spiritual seeker with community, access to a tradition and to sustained teaching, a shared life-style, and companionship on his/her spiritual journey. It is, in a way, a pioneering effort to preserve tradition while adapting to a new situation.

FEATURES FOR DISCERNMENT

- Distinctive in its intention to respect primacy of lay vocation while handing on monastic tradition
- Lay contemplative community
- Strong emphasis on monastic symbol and ritual
- Highly structured and scholarly formation program for members
- Highly qualified academic and spiritual leader and teacher

■ SCHOLA CONTEMPLATIONIS *(School for Contemplation)*

Address: 3425 Forest Lane
         Pfafftown, North Carolina 27040-9545

Type of Contemplative Formation Model: International Network

Founder: Beatrice Bruteau

Editors: Beatrice Bruteau and James Somerville

Tradition: Christian, Vedantic, Jewish

Sources: Judeo-Christian; Eastern and Western mysticism

Start-up Date: February 1984

Participant Profile: The Schola is composed mostly of married people, with some religious, clergy and students. Average age is about thirty-eight to forty-two years. Women comprise sixty percent of the total associate population and men forty percent. Most of the associates are well educated; some are writers and other professionals. A substantial number are Anglican clergy. The predominant religious denomination is Catholic in the broad sense of the term.

Newsletter: *The Roll* carries letters and articles by associates, announcements, book reviews, miscellaneous items of interest to contemplatives. It has a current distribution of six hundred and fifty readers and is distributed in most states in the United States and most Canadian Provinces, Western Europe, with a scattering in Africa, Asia and Australia.

Programs: Occasional retreats for associates

Cost: Nothing required. Most associates donate $15-$25 a year to defray cost of printing/posting *The Roll*.

The Schola Contemplationis (The School for Contemplation) and its magazine-newsletter, *The Roll*, had their origins at a retreat for contemplatives at Maggie Valley's Living Waters Retreat Center in 1984. The Schola has as its primary goal "to acquaint people interested in the contemplative path with one another" and to offer them encouragement and support. The main work of the Schola is carried out through *The Roll*, which started out as a round robin letter among the participants of the Maggie Valley retreat in 1984. *The Roll* has evolved, over its fifteen-year history, into a forty-page quarterly that offers its readership a share in the scholarly and inspiring contemplative writing of Beatrice Bruteau, James Somerville and many other people. In addition there are varied contributions—all of interest to the contemplative—from several of its reader-associates, a number of whom are writers, professionals, religious men and women.

The editors of *The Roll*, Beatrice Bruteau and James Somerville, select material for publication as well as respond to correspondence connected with the quarterly.

Although Schola associates subscribe to *The Roll*, anyone else is welcome to receive the quarterly. While there is no set fee, voluntary donations toward printing and mailing costs are welcomed. The average donation is between $15 to $25. The editors receive no compensation for their work. In addition to publication of *The Roll*, the Schola offers occasional retreats for its associates. Some seminars and discussion groups centered around the Pfafftown, North Carolina, area have also had a loose affiliation with the Schola. This School of Contemplation has no residential community. It is more properly considered a network that enables contemplatives to connect with one another on a more informal basis. Its associates are not recruited in any way but rather are ordinarily drawn to the School by word of mouth. The rich content of its quarterly serves as a primary means of acquainting its readers with the benefits of this type of association.

FEATURES FOR DISCERNMENT

- A largely literary program; offers rich and scholarly magazine-newsletter
- No residential community
- Loose affiliation with other contemplatives
- Occasional retreats with other associates

PART FOUR

APPENDICES

What Do You Mean by Contemplation?

(Responses From Leaders at Various Sites)

One of the questions the research team posed to the directors and founders of the places of contemplative formation that they visited was, "What do you mean by contemplation?" Below are some of the varied responses:

> "Awareness inward and outward and giving oneself to that awareness."
> *Christina Spahn, Center for Action and Contemplation*

> "A reconstituted sense of the self (the image of the vine and the branches). The thing that comes from that...living out of the contemplative space choicefully, consciously...."
> *Father Richard Rohr, Center for Action and Contemplation*

> "How we look at creation, people and events of every day... that comes from God, our Source, leading us in how to see the world."
> *Sister Margaret Williams, Desert House of Prayer*

> "Gift of wisdom—taste, knowledge of God; consciousness of the Presence of God."
> *Father John Kane, Desert House of Prayer*

> "Presence to this *now*, presence to Presence, spousal prayer."
> *Sister Therese Sedlock, O.S.F., Our Lady of Solitude*
> *Contemplative House of Prayer*

"Deep relationship with God—so deep it is like breathing air: one doesn't know one does it."
Dean Margaret Fraser, Pendle Hill

"Inner communion with the Lord, awareness of the Presence, going beyond thought, being in the Presence."
Sister Pascaline Coff, Osage Monastery

"Communion with God; oneness with the Divine."
Jennifer Sullivan, Shantivanam

"A long loving look at the Real, with eyes closed or not."
Father Joseph Nassal, Shantivanam

"Conscious awareness of oneness with God. In the ordinary person's life, it's a gradual realization. The gift is: we begin to realize."
Ginny Manss, Association of Contemplative Sisters

"Experience beyond words."
Father Warren McCarthy, Christian Meditation Center

"The person in whom slowly over a lifetime there grows up within more and more vibrantly the image of God. Because of this, the image or likeness within calls to the likeness without."
Sister Constance FitzGerald, Summer Seminar on Carmelite Spirituality

"Two answers: Inflow of God into the substance of the soul (John of the Cross); purely passive, when we are made available and pure of heart. Second, what we do in order to have that openness and purity. God does not fit in an occupied heart (John of the Cross)."
Mary Jo Meadows, Resources for Ecumenical Spirituality

"Imageless prayer."
Sister Barbara Hazzard, Hesed Community

"Sitting face to face with the Beloved."
Father Isaiah, New Camaldoli Hermitage

"Receptive and attentive attitude of consciousness. Unitive experience—one, single, before division. You know what you are by being."
Father Bruno Barnhart, New Camaldoli Hermitage

"Let the talking to God develop to rest in God's Presence; come to a stage in which we rest in the encirclement of God."
Father Michael Buckley, Secular Order of Discalced Carmelites

"There is a contemplative thrust or orientation within by virtue of one's very existence; it is part of being. Contemplative prayer is a presence, 'here I am'—wordless, imageless, loving surrender."
Sister Marie Coombs, Lebh Shomea

"Being present to the Real, to Reality, to the Mystery, to God. Open to the presence of God, of the Sacred."
Michael Johnson, Cistercian Lay Contemplatives

"Resting in God as in the fourth phase of *lectio divina*."
Rev. Don Bredthauer, Academy for Spiritual Formation

"Silent listening, to everything, and how I respond."
Theonia Amenda, Academy for Spiritual Formation

"The contemplative life is a life devoted to seeing Reality and rejoicing in it. It's a whole life-style.... The contemplative feels that nothing is in the territory of the so-called profane; everything is sacred, everything is full of divine life and value. The supreme goal of your life is to see Reality, to absorb Reality and then contribute to the ongoing process of reality."
Beatrice Bruteau, Fellowship of the Holy Trinity

"Pastorally, we meditate on things of God either through sacred reading or devotions, or by simply enjoying God's creation. Then quite effortlessly, we pass over into passive contemplation, where God is experienced in himself beyond any external form or idea."
John Michael Talbot, Little Portion Hermitage

What Do People Want in a Program for Lay Contemplative Formation?

A Summary of Responses to a 1992 ACS Survey

In 1992 and 1994 the Association of Contemplative Sisters received a small grant from the Lilly Endowment to conduct and collate a survey of its members regarding programs for lay contemplative formation. A task force was formed, consisting of Mary Frohlich, Judy Fulcher, Ginny Manss, Jan Strong, Wendy Wright and Sue Zilisch. The task force met several times to formulate, administer and report the survey.

One of the survey questions asked ACS members to articulate what they are looking for in a formation program. No prompting suggestions were provided; people were left free to respond in any way according to their own insights and priorities. About 120 people filled in this part of the survey. Some of them wrote only a few words; others wrote essays. This brief report collates and reflects on these responses.

First, a word about the limitations of this report. Our survey was not done in a "scientific" manner; people were simply asked a broad question to which they could reply in any form. When it came time to do the collating, three task force members (Mary Frohlich, Judy Fulcher and Sue Zilisch) divided up the response sheets and summarized responses as we found appropriate. Finally, Mary took these summaries and—with frequent references back to the original sheets—did the final totalling and organizing. Still later, in preparation for this book, Mary revised the materials and added some additional commentary.

This is clearly not "quantitative" research, which would involve the use of precise questions, quantifiable responses and statistical reporting. Nor does it fulfill professional standards for "qualitative" research, which would demand carefully designed questions administered to a clearly delimited research population. Thus, while the report may give a fairly good sense of what people's concerns are, it should by no means be construed as a definitive statement.

It is noteworthy that a large percentage of the responses expressed strong appreciation for the fact that the issue of formation for lay contemplatives is being addressed, as well as hope that the overall research project would help to fill a gap that has been so painful for many. In that spirit we offer this report, with all its imperfections.

I. CONCERNS ABOUT ORIENTATION, TRADITION OR VISION

Seventy-seven responses made comments that dealt in some way with a concern about a formation program's general orientation.

a. Christian orientation (total: 62)
- Christian, but also incorporates insights/practices of other world religions (10)
- Christian (4)
- Based in Scripture and gospel values (40)
- Orthodoxy and balance in relation to Christian tradition (3)
- Based in Catholic Church and doctrine (3)
- Ecumenical—includes all Christian denominations (2)

b. Balance of tradition and freshness (total: 18)
- Teaches classic masters and traditions (11)
- Teaches current as well as past masters (5)
- Balance of rooting in history and new directions (2)

c. Clarity of vision (total: 13)
- Clarity about what orientation or tradition it is rooted in (8)
- Has a vision (3)
- Clarity about its understanding of contemplative prayer (2)

d. Other desirable aspects of orientation (total: 20)

- Feminist thinking (9)
- Diversity (7)
- Avoid "New Age" and other bizarre approaches (2)
- Creation spirituality as center (1)
- Not overly "ecclesiocentric" (1)

A significant number of people brought up, without prompting, a desire for an explicitly Christian orientation. It should be noted that our research population consisted of persons of Christian—in fact, largely Roman Catholic—heritage, although some may regard themselves as "post-Christian" at this point. Many of these respondents expressed a desire also to be exposed to the contemplative traditions of other world religions. Concerns for a balance of the "old" and the "new," as well as the desire for a program to manifest clarity of vision, were also significant.

II. CHARACTERISTICS OF LEADERS OR DIRECTORS

Sixty responses gave input on what background and qualities are desired in those who will lead a program of lay contemplative formation.

- Spiritual directors rooted in contemplative prayer (24)
- Training, expertise, learning on part of directors (21)
- Holiness, integrity, competency of leaders (9)
- Both female and male leaders (2)
- Leaders trained in psychology and mental health (2)
- Strong leadership (1)
- Leaders are religious, preferably vowed (1)

It is clear that a major concern of our respondents is the spiritual preparation and authenticity of of those who will guide them. As task force member Wendy Wright put it at one of our meetings, people are looking for "Ammas and Abbas"—women and men of deep contemplation and wisdom.

III. PROVISION OF HUMAN SUPPORT THROUGH SPIRITUAL DIRECTION, COMMUNITY AND ONGOING CONTACT

Sixty-four responses referred to specific needs and desires for support and guidance on the human level, through spiritual direction, companionship, faith sharing, community life and/or long-term support.

a. Includes spiritual direction (total: 13)

- A spiritual director, mentor or "master" relationship is provided (6)
- Personal direction and help in discerning one's call (5)
- Guidance on finding and developing a relation with a spiritual director (1)
- Includes both individual and group spiritual direction (1)

b. Includes human relationships and community experience (total: 30)

- Includes a community experience of living contemplatively (7)
- Shared prayer and liturgy (4)
- Evident emphasis on love of neighbor (4)
- Sharing of experiences (3)
- Based in an ongoing community (3)
- Participants are accountable to others, not "lone rangers" (3)
- Silence together as well as sharing (2)
- "Family-style" instead of institutional (2)
- Develops listening skills for small and large groups as well as one-on-one (1)
- Monasteries open to lay people living in, with additional association and formation outside the monastery (1)

c. Includes ongoing support (total: 21)

- Follow-up with periodic meetings for support, sharing, prayer, etc. (14)
- Includes ongoing sharing with others; "support groups" (3)
- Gathering in community at least once a year (1)
- Ongoing spiritual direction (1)
- Program that can be repeated (1)
- Ongoing study (1)

In addition to the longing for holy and experienced spiritual directors, many of our respondents have a clear sense of the need for other forms of human support. A significant number specifically called for formation to take place in a community format and to include opportunities for various forms of spiritual sharing. The need for long-term support, relationships and guidance is also a significant theme.

IV. EVIDENCE OF SPIRITUAL AUTHENTICITY

Forty-four responses dealt with issues related to the quality of spirituality manifested in the program.

a. Soundness and depth of spirituality (total: 28)
- Sound theology and spirituality (12)
- Gospel values and simplicity (5)
- Depth in wisdom traditions of great Christian contemplatives (3)
- Encourages spiritual growth through prayer (3)
- Helps one grow in self-knowledge and radical surrender (3)
- One knows it is a "safe place" (1)
- It has "the ring of the genuine" (1)

b. Openness, flexibility, freedom (total: 16)
- Open, creative and flexible; not "cookie cutter" (4)
- Flexibility according to individual experience and need (4)
- Open to God's direction of the individual (3)
- Respect for uniqueness and privacy needs of individual (3)
- Sense of freedom and humility (1)
- Common sense or the desire for it (1)

The previously mentioned longing for holy and experienced guides carries over to the qualities desired in the entire program. Our respondents clearly have an "eagle eye" for spirituality that is authentic and—in that sense—rigorous. At the same time they are very concerned that there be an attitude of openness, flexibility and common sense rather than a rigid formula applied to all persons and circumstances.

V. EVIDENCE OF HOLISTIC SPIRITUALITY

Fifty-one respondents referred to the desire for a spirituality that offers balance and integration in regard to prayer, work, global justice and psychological health.

a. Balance of prayer and activity (total: 16)
- Balances and integrates prayer and everyday life (7)
- Not a problem to have an outside job, even in a residential contemplative community (4)
- Does not require separation from one's everyday setting (2)
- Balance of prayer and other activities (1)
- Prayer and ministry are connected (1)
- Adaptability to lay life (1)

b. Awareness of larger world issues (total: 18)
- Includes ecological and global perspective (6)
- Aware of current events; not separated from "world" (4)
- Peace and justice awareness (4)
- Consciously works against racism (2)
- Practices listening to God in the lives of the poor (1)
- Community provides for itself instead of living on donations (1)

c. Psychological health and sensitivity (total: 17)
- Holistic; the whole person taken into consideration (8)
- Knowledgeable about psychology, dysfunctions, etc. (4)
- Program is stable, emotionally sound, etc. (2)
- Covers psychology and spirituality of "dark nights" (1)
- Not fundamentally therapeutic (1)
- Does not place emphasis on mystical phenomena (1)

This set of concerns points toward desire for a spirituality that in no sense turns away from "the world," the body and secular responsibilities. For lay contemplatives, the need and desire to integrate action and contemplation is clear. Our respondents also have social justice concerns and see this as important in their manifestation of the contemplative life. They are sensitive to questions of psychological health, and recognize the need for a program to deal explicitly and responsibly with these in order to foster the fullness of spiritual growth.

VI. OTHER DESIRED ASPECTS OF CONTENT OR STRUCTURE

This category includes a variety of specific interests that were not summed up within the earlier sections (73 responses).

a. Silence and solitude (total: 21)

- Adequate time for silence and solitude (17)
- Retreats offered (2)
- Private rooms (2)

b. Experiential approach (total: 15)

- Experiential approach primary; intellectual study serves it (12)
- Not "workshops," but a full-fledged experience of contemplative living; an "apprenticeship" (3)

c. Training in contemplative prayer (total: 15)

- Clear training in how to pray (5)
- Some history and theory of kinds of contemplative prayer (4)
- Exposure to various contemplative traditions (3)
- Solid method of meditation (2)
- One classic discipline in depth, instead of eclectic approach (1)

d. Good input (total: 10)

- Reliable training in contemporary Catholic theology, pastoral care, etc. (5)
- Good background in Scripture and theology (4)
- Good speakers and input (1)

e. Discipline (total: 4)

- Discipline (2)
- A rule of life (2)

f. Other desirable aspects (total: 8)

- Daily mass with an ordained Roman Catholic priest (2)
- Body work (yoga, dance, movement, running, etc.) (2)
- Devotion to Mary and the Rosary (1)
- Holistic health and organic medicine awareness (1)
- Dream work and other "inner work" (1)
- Journaling (1)

VII. THE CREDENTIALS, BACKGROUND AND REFERENCES OF THE PROGRAM

Fourteen responses referred to the value of having good information and references about a potential program.

- Good track record; well recommended; good reputation (6)
- Opportunity to interview previous participants (6)
- Sponsored by an ongoing, stable, permanent group (1)
- Opportunity for trial visit (1)

VIII. LOCATION, ACCESSIBILITY, COST, ETC., OF A PROGRAM

Twenty-seven responses mentioned concrete concerns that would affect their ability to participate in a program.

a. Who can participate (total: 22)

- Availability to average person in terms of time, costs, etc. (12)
- Clear information given about time requirements (5)
- Various levels of entrance, for those with more or less background (2)
- Screening for participants (1)
- Open to all (1)
- No age limits (1)

b. Geographical issues (total: 5)

- Geographical location (3)
- Isolated natural setting (1)
- Accessiblity by public transportation (1)

The questions of inclusiveness and especially of cost were important to a number of our respondents. They emphasized that programs need to provide good preparatory information to potential participants, as well as appropriate screening. A few also had specific interests in relation to the location of the program, such as that it be close by or that it be in a natural setting.

■ SUMMARY

Some of the most striking findings of this survey include:

- The largest number of responses focus on the desire for holy, experienced, well-trained spiritual guides.
- A related theme is the awareness that contemplative formation requires a base in relationships and community. Solitude and silence are high values, but so are sharing and mutual support.
- There is a great longing for a spirituality that clearly manifests its authenticity and that is well-grounded in theology and classic traditions.
- Those surveyed are quite committed to the idea that a contemporary contemplative spirituality should be one that balances contemplation and action, maintains involvement in larger world issues and is psychologically astute.
- Many express the sense that contemplative formation must be flexible, open, creative—and that ultimately, it is God who "directs" the truly contemplative individual.
- A Christian orientation is central for our constituency, but a significant number want this integrated with practices from other world religions.

In reviewing the report, the task force noted that while this provides an interesting snapshot of the lay contemplative movement, we would not want to have it construed as "market research" intended to help someone develop a program to match "consumer demand." Rather, we see it as a way of trying to listen to where the Spirit is moving among the People of God. A group that is thinking about developing a program for contemplative formation needs to balance the freshness of that kind of listening with attentiveness to the deep wisdom enshrined in living contemplative traditions and in the best of contemporary theology. While the contemplative journey will never be a completely "smooth ride," we can rightfully aspire to make the gifts we have received a bit more readily accessible to the next generation.

List of Contributors

Mary Bookser, S.C., is director of initial formation for the Sisters of Charity of Cincinnati. She is an adjunct professor of religious studies at the College of Mount Saint Joseph and the studies in spirituality program in the greater Cincinnati region.

Kathryn Damiano is one of the founders and leaders of "The School of the Spirit" ministry. This project of Philadelphia Yearly Meeting of the Religious Society of Friends conducts a variety of programs for contemplatives and spiritual nurturers.

Ann G. Denham is a former United Methodist minister who became a Roman Catholic on her contemplative journey. A writer and teacher, she is involved in various local groups, particularly her parish and the Association of Contemplative Sisters. Ann and her husband, Walter, live in Sacramento, California.

Mark and Ruth Dundon are active members of the "Centering Prayer" movement. Their home is in Bardstown, Kentucky.

Robert Durback is editor of *Seeds of Hope: A Henri Nouwen Reader*, (Doubleday, 1997) and a contributor to "The Spiritual Formation Bible" (Zondervan, 1999). His articles have appeared in *Catholic Digest, Praying, Spiritual Life* and *America*.

Tilden Edwards is founder and director of the Shalem Institute for Spiritual Formation in Bethesda, Maryland, an international center for contemplative spirituality. He is the author of seven books in the area of contemplative practice, leadership and spiritual direction, the latest being *Tending the Soul* (Paulist Press, 2000).

Mary Frohlich, H.M., is assistant professor of spirituality at Catholic Theological Union in Chicago. She is the author of *Praying with Scripture* (Center for Learning, 1993) and *The Intersubjectivity of the Mystic* (Scholars Press, 1993), as well as numerous articles. She recently joined the Sisters of the Humility of Mary (Villa Maria, Pennsylvania).

Deborah A. Gephardt is a homemaker, wife, mother and grandmother. She has long been involved in volunteer work. As part of her inner journey, she traveled to India, experiencing life's contemplative dimension in the ashram of Father Bede Griffiths and its active dimension in Calcutta in Mother Teresa's Home for the Dying and Destitutes.

Stephen K. Hatch leads the Contemplative Center of Fort Collins, Colorado. He frequently gives retreats and workshops emphasizing the relation between the contemplative life and earth spirituality. He has an eclectic religious background which has included elements of Baptist, charismatic, Quaker, Catholic, Buddhist and American Indian spiritualities. Stephen is currently writing a book about finding the masculine and feminine aspects of the Divine in a love affair with the landscape. He is married and the father of two teen-aged daughters.

Robert A. Jonas is founder and director of The Empty Bell, a center for Christian and Zen spirituality in Watertown, Massachusetts. He is currently completing a book manuscript on his travels with his *shakuhachi* (Japanese flute).

Virginia Manss is a member of a small lay contemplative community. From 1992 to 1996 Ginny was the elected president of the Association of Contemplative Sisters. After serving as an administrator for non-profit organizations for several years, she currently balances her contemplative life-style with part-time work at the Carmelite Monastery in Indianapolis, Indiana.

Barbara E. Scott is a hospital and hospice chaplain, as well as a bereavement coordinator. She was president of the Association of Contemplative Sisters for 1996-98. She resides in the north woods of Wisconsin.

Wendy M. Wright is professor of spirituality at Creighton University in Omaha, Nebraska. An acknowledged expert in Salesian studies, she has written extensively in this area as well as on other topics in spirituality. She coedited *Silent Fire: An Invitation to Western Mysticism* (Harper & Row) and authored *Sacred Dwelling: A Spirituality of Family Life* (Crossroad) and three books on the liturgical year: *The Vigil, The Rising, The Time Between* (Upper Room). Wendy is married and has two daughters and a son.

■ PROJECT SPONSOR

The Association of Contemplative Sisters was founded in 1969 as a meeting ground, support system and advocacy group for members of canonically established Roman Catholic contemplative communities of women. In 1986 membership was opened to all contemplative women. National meetings occur every other summer. Five regional meetings (Eastern, New England, Mideast, Midwest and Western) take place during the alternate summers. There are also some local clusters that meet more frequently. For information about membership, contact the current president.

■ INDEX OF FORMATION SITES